IDEOLOGY AND POPULAR PROTEST

Ideology and Popular Protest

by

GEORGE RUDÉ

Pantheon Books, New York

LIBRARY OF CONGRESS CATALOGING IN PUBLICATION DATA

Rudé, George F. E.
Ideology and popular protest.

Bibliography: p.
Includes index.
1. Revolutions—History.   2. Social movements—
History.   3. Ideology.   I. Title.
HM281.R8   303.6'4'09   80-8030
ISBN 0-394-51372-x
ISBN 0-394-73966-3 (pbk.)

Contents

Introduction

The purpose of this introduction is to attempt to explain to the reader, as briefly as I can, what led me to write this book and why it has taken the form that it has.

In my earlier work, I have often been concerned with establishing the identity (or 'faces') of the common people in history that have taken part in demonstrations, riots and revolutions occurring mainly in a 'pre-industrial society' – that is, at a time when today's industrial society' with its major division into employers and workers, capitalists and proletarians, was still in the process of formation. So, initially, I was largely concerned with the question 'who' which I felt had been inadequately considered by earlier writers of history or social science. And from this initial concern there inevitably developed the further question *why* did people act as they did, what prompted them to riot or rebel, what were the motives that impelled them? This concern with motivation led me further to attempt to distinguish between the long and the short term and to draw a dividing line between 'social-economic' and 'political' factors and to attempt to explain how the two became related and merged in such movements as that of the *sans-culottes* in the French Revolution or of the Londoners that shouted for Wilkes and burned down Roman Catholic chapels and schools in the riots of the 1760s to 1780.

But, as I have come to realize, the study of *motives* – even when some attention is paid to such elusive concepts as N. J. Smelser's 'generalized beliefs' – is an unsatisfactory one in itself, as it tends to present the problem in a piecemeal fashion and fails to do justice to the full range of ideas or beliefs that underlie social and political action, whether of old-style rulers, 'rising' bourgeois or of 'inferior' social groups.

This underlying body of ideas is what I here term the 'ideology of protest' (whether popular or other). Some will find such a definition far too woolly and wide-ranging and may – if they should chance to read the book – accuse me of using a

catch-as-catch-can phrase where a stricter and a far more specific definition is required. How (it may be said) can an author
professing to be a Marxist extend the use of the term 'ideology'
so far beyond the limitations placed on it by Marx and Engels
and by subsequent scholars of repute, both Marxists and
others? It is true enough that Marx began by restricting its use to
'the ideas of the ruling class' (particularly of the bourgeoisie)
and saw it as a weapon of class rule, as an important means
whereby that class exercised its domination (or hegemony) over
the subordinate classes in society. But he also opened the door
to a wider definition by noting that the proletariat, in order to
achieve power, had to go beyond the 'false reality' imposed on it
by its rulers and to develop a 'true' or 'class' consciousness of its
own. But Marx and Engels were writing (as they showed most
clearly in the *Communist Manifesto*) of a society in the course of
polarization between the two major contending classes of
capitalists and proletarians, and they therefore assumed that the
older 'traditional' classes or social groups – the peasants, shopkeepers, handicraftsmen and the like – would become absorbed
in the process and that, in the meantime, such 'ideology' as
they continued to possess would lose any identity of its own
and merely reflect that of one or other of the two major classes
struggling for control of the state. There are, however, indi-
cations in Marx's and Engels's later work that they had not
intended that, even in a developing industrial society where
'polarization' lay at the end of the road, there should be no
room at all left for other intermediate forms of ideology; in
short, the 'theory' that Marx later wrote of as 'gripping' the
masses could not be solely measured in terms of its conformity
to a 'true' or a 'false' consciousness.[1]* Yet it has been in these
terms of a rigid antithesis between the two extremes that several
later Marxist scholars – among whom Georg Lukács – has
played a prominent role – have discussed the ideological
development of the working class in modern society.

Yet, in some countries such as Italy, in which, alongside a
growing industrialization, the peasants have continued to play a
significant role, it was inevitable that Marxist scholars should be
found to challenge the sharpness of such an antithesis; this was
particularly to be the case after Italy's 'failed' revolution of the

---

* See notes at end of each chapter.

early 1920s which could only too obviously be attributed to the workers' (and their party's) failure to make any serious attempt to persuade the peasants to lend support to their cause. Antonio Gramsci, who had been a major participant in those events, reflected on this failure and its deeper causes while a prisoner of Mussolini and wrote down his conclusions, together with much else, in his *Prison Letters* and *Prison Notebooks* (both published many years after his death). Writing of the workers' need to counter the hegemony of their rulers by developing an ideology of their own, he insisted that attention must be paid to the ideological needs of the 'traditional' classes of peasants and craftsmen; and from this he argued further that attention must also be paid to the simpler and less structured ideas circulating among the common people, often 'contradictory' and confused and compounded of folklore, myth and day-to-day popular experience. So ideology and consciousness, in his view, no longer remained the sole preserve of the two main protagonists in modern society (Gramsci calls them the 'fundamental' classes), but are extended to embrace the 'traditional' classes, including the common people other than those engaged in industrial production, as well.

Now if it is reasonable (as I think it is) that Gramsci, in writing of ideology, should make provision for wider social groups in an industrial country of the twentieth century – though, admittedly, one in which the peasants continue to be of enormous importance – how much more must it be so when an author is writing not of an industrial, but of a 'pre-industrial', society in which the two major classes dividing society today were still, if they existed at all, in the process of formation! It is evident, in fact, that in writing of such a society, such terms as 'true' or 'false' consciousness (that Marx had originally applied to the industrial working class) can have no relevance at all.

But merely to extend the definition of the term 'ideology' to include the 'inherent' and traditional ideas, or attitudes, of the common people is neither original (John Plamenatz, among non-Marxist writers on the subject, has done the same), nor is it adequate for the purpose I have in mind. Gramsci writes of the need to analyse ideology 'historically',[2] but he does not go on to show how the 'non-organic ideology' (roughly corresponding to my own use of the term 'inherent ideas') of the 'popular' or 'traditional' classes are related to or become merged with the more structured or sophisticated ideas of the 'fundamental' classes of which he writes. Nor is there any reason why he should, as it would add little to the discussion of 'hegemony' that mainly concerns him. But, in writing of the popular ideology of *protest*, it is essential that I should know how that ideology is composed and how *historically* its components have come together. This is not important in such actions as food riots or machine-breaking or in more or less spontaneous acts of peasant rebellion, in which the wage-earners, small consumers or peasants carry through their actions of protest with the aid of their own ideological resources alone. But in the case of revolutions, or of peasant or consumers' rebellions set in the context of revolution, the picture is a very different one. For in such cases the 'inherent' ideology (as I shall explain in my second chapter) is not sufficient and the native or traditional ideology of the common people requires to be wedded to and merge with an ideology or a 'theory' (to repeat Marx's term) of a more sophisticated and more 'forward-looking' kind coming from 'without' – that is, from a higher social group; and we shall see what happened when the craftsmen and shopkeepers of Revolutionary Paris absorbed and adapted the explosive ideas that their political mentors, the bourgeoisie, had inherited in turn from Enlightenment writers like Montesquieu and Rousseau.

The first Part of my book deals with the development of such a 'theory' of an ideology of protest, beginning with its origins in Marx and Engels and as later adapted to industrial society, each in his own manner, by Lukács and Gramsci; and, in a second chapter, with my own formulation of the theory as related to popular protest movements occurring in predominantly 'pre-industrial' times. Parts Two to Four apply the 'theory', as I conceive it, to a number of 'pre-industrial' situations: to Peasants (in various countries and at various times) in Part Two and in Part Three Revolutions (ranging from the English revolution of the seventeenth century to the last of the French revolutions in 1871); while Part Four strikes out on a course of its own, following the development of the style and ideology of popular protest in England from the eighteenth and early nineteenth centuries to the industrial society of the 1850s onwards. Moreover, the last of the 'English' chapters, being concerned with the entirely new problems of an industrial society, is rapidly sketched and leaves readers to puzzle out for themselves the answer to the question, 'What next?'

NOTES

1. 'Theory . . . becomes a material force as soon as it has gripped the masses' (K. Marx, Introduction to 'Contribution to the Critique of Hegel's Philosophy of Law', *Collected Works*, 3, p. 182).
2. *Selections from the Prison Notebooks of Antonio Gramsci*, ed. Q. Hoare and G. Nowell Smith, London, 1971, p. 371.

Part One

IDEOLOGY AND CLASS CONSCIOUSNESS

1

Ideology and Class Consciousness

The study of ideology as an instrument of struggle and social change began with Marx. The notion of ideology as a philosophical concept, however, goes back more than a half-century before to the *philosophes* of the Enlightenment in France. One of these, the materialist Helvétius, while not actually using the term, prepared the way for its use in his phrase, 'our ideas are the necessary consequences of the societies in which we live'. The term, in fact, only entered the language of philosophy a generation later, when the latter-day *philosophes* of the Revolution used the Institut de France, created by the Directory in 1795, to propagate the rational traditions of the Enlightenment. It was one of these, Antoine Destutt de Tracy, who, a few years later, coined the word 'ideology' to apply to the theory of ideas in general.[1]

The term reappears, but now as an idiom of German idealist philosophy, in the writings of Kant and Hegel a dozen years after. To Hegel mind was the 'universal agent' of history and (in his words) 'what manifests itself to philosophic thought is the history of mind – veiled by its embodiment in matter, but still plainly discernible as the motive force of the universal process'. Ideology, in this context, was a direct projection of mind ('objective mind', as he wrote) without any separate identity. Moreover, as 'ideology' was a universal concept, there was no question of its being seen to serve the purpose of any particular class or group, let alone of the masses who, to the idealist philosophers, were a matter of small concern.[2]

Marx and Engels, as is known, served their philosophical apprenticeship with Hegel; among the debts they owed him were their continuing belief in the universality of truth, the unity of mankind, and the philosophical notion of 'alienation'; above all, they made their own his dialectical method which saw progress as the outcome of conflict through the interplay of opposites, of 'thesis' and 'antithesis'. But, at first hesitantly, they began in the early 1840s to turn his philosophy 'upside down' by rejecting his idealism and substituting the notion of the primacy of matter for Hegel's conception of mind as the active and primary agent of history. This reversal of loyalties was first publicly made manifest in *The Holy Family*, which they wrote and published jointly in early 1845. 'History' [in Hegel], they wrote, 'like truth, becomes a person apart, a metaphysical subject, of which the real individuals are merely the bearers'; and further: 'Hegel's conception of History presupposes an abstract or absolute spirit which develops in such a way that Humanity is nothing but a mass which more or less consciously bears it along.'[3] And in the place of this metaphysical view of history, Marx and Engels countered with their recently adopted notion of 'historical materialism'.[4] In *The German Ideology*, written a few months later, they explain its underlying principle at first tentatively – as follows: 'Life is not determined by consciousness but consciousness by life'; and, moreover, this new view of history 'does not explain practice from the idea but explains the formation of ideas from material practice'.[5]

This materialist reversal of Hegel derives, it will be noticed, in part at least from Helvétius's notion of the subjection of ideas to the societies out of which they sprang. But with an important difference: to Marx this subjection was by no means absolute or one-sided, and there was a delicate interaction between the two. As he wrote in *The German Ideology*: 'Circumstances make men as much as men make circumstances';[6] and, more fully, in the *Theses on Feuerbach*, written soon after: 'The materialist doctrine that men are products of circumstances and upbringing . . . forgets that it is men who change circumstances and that the educator himself needs to be educated.'[7] Thus Marx and Engels, far from having fully shed Hegel's philosophical influence, defend Hegel's dialectical method against its total rejection by the 'vulgar materialism' of Feuerbach and his associates. But, while stressing man's ability to 'change circumstances', Marx places strict temporal limits on his capacity to do so: 'Mankind', he writes in another famous phrase, 'only sets itself goals that it can solve.'[8]

And so we come, by this unavoidably roundabout way, to Marx's notion of ideology. (We can hardly call it a theory, as it is nowhere comprehensively formulated as is the case with his theory of history.) It comes first squarely into his vision, and line of fire, when he and Engels are deeply engaged in battle with Hegel's currently most vocal disciples, the Young Hegelians. Thus, as their 'upside-down' vision of the world is a false one, so ideology, which plays so large a part in their thinking, becomes a 'false consciousness' which projects a 'false reality'. With those duped by the new German philosophy in mind, he writes: 'Hitherto men have constantly made up for themselves false conceptions about themselves, about what they are and what they ought to be.' But none so much as the German middle class under the influence of the new philosophy:

> These innocent and childlike fancies are the kernel of the modern Young-Hegelian philosophy . . . the first volume of the present publication has the aim of uncloaking these sheep . . . (and) of showing how their bleating merely imitates in a philosophic form the conceptions of the German middle class. . . .[9]

So his notion of ideology, whether of the post-Hegelian kind or any other, got off to a bad start.

However, these 'fancies' had, as Marx tells us in the same volume, another side as well: they served as a useful weapon of class rule. 'The ideas of the ruling class,' he writes, ' are in every epoch the ruling ideas, i.e. the class which is the ruling *material* force of society is at the same time its ruling *intellectual* force'; and a part of this domination evidently consisted in imposing its own fantasies and 'false reality' on the subject class – that is, in the modern industrial society in which Marx and Engels were mainly concerned, on the proletariat.

But it would hardly have accorded with Marx's belief in the historic role of the proletariat as the future 'grave-digger' of capitalism to conceive that it, too, was capable of having no more than a 'false consciousness' and of limiting its vision to no more than a 'false reality'. On the contrary, to end its subjection and break through the 'false reality' that capitalism had imposed on it, the proletariat – and it was the only class capable of doing so – must develop a 'true' consciousness, or class consciousness, peculiar to itself. In this way alone it would become aware of its subjection and learn how to overcome it. But such an awakening would not be an easy one, nor would it be a piecemeal process in which individual proletarians would simply see the light and pass it on to others. It would be an essentially class phenomenon, though the means by which it would happen was at first left very much in doubt. According to Marx's earliest formulation (which still strongly bears the stamp of Hegelian philosophy):

> It is not a question of what this or that proletarian, or even the whole proletariat, *regards* as its aim. It is a question of *what the proletariat is* and what, in accordance with this *being*, it will be historically compelled to do.[10]

But that, even at this comparatively early stage of his 'liberation' from Hegel, Marx did not think of this as a sudden or 'total' revelation that would carry the whole proletariat forward at a leap is evident from a sentence that follows soon after: 'There is no need to explain here that a large part of the English and French proletariat is already *conscious* of its historic task and is constantly working to develop that consciousness into complete clarity.'[11]

And how was that fuller 'clarity' to be attained? It is evident that Marx and Engels, although they never formulated a list of priorities in this regard, attached a major importance to participation in class struggle, both political and economic, with both short-term and long-term objectives in view. 'The Communists,' runs the *Manifesto of the Communist Party*, 'fight for the immediate aims, for the enforcement of momentary interests of the working class; but in the movement of the present, they also represent and take care of the future of that movement.'[12] And if, as we saw earlier, it was man's 'material being' that determined his consciousness, how far could that consciousness in turn serve to develop the economic base – how far, in fact, could the 'superstructure' (of which consciousness was a part) assume a degree of independence and alter the base from which it sprang? This becomes an endless conundrum and has been a hotly debated theme, susceptible to varying interpretations since Marx first penned his famous phrase in the *Critique of Political Economy*. Taken literally, the formulation he then used would appear to justify those 'determinists' – *and* critics of Marx – who have insisted that the 'superstructure' (including consciousness and ideas) must, according to Marxist theory, be a mere and a direct reflection of the base from which it emanates. Others, however, have argued that ideas and ideology, while in the first instance owing their existence to man's material being, can at crucial moments in history, assume, temporarily at least, an almost independent role. While Marx's earlier 'philosophical' formulations were either ambivalent or appeared to favour the first interpretation, there seems little doubt that both Marx's and Engels's historical writing – *The Eighteenth Brumaire* and *Peasant War in Germany*, for instance – lend support to the second. Marx himself, in a later passage, claimed that 'theory becomes a material force when it grips the masses',[13] which might appear to clinch the matter; but Engels, writing after Marx's death, felt it necessary to re-state their views. In doing so, he conceded that in the heat of their duels with their philosophical opponents, they had probably overstated their case, but insisted that 'ultimately' or in the final analysis ideas and religion and other forms of the 'superstructure' draw their existence from the material base.[14] As it is impossible, however, to mark the exact point where the 'final analysis' takes over, the debate inevitably continues.

We must return briefly to the question of how that fuller 'clarity' of consciousness of which Marx wrote in *The Holy Family* might be attained. As we have seen, the *Manifesto* places the main emphasis on participation; but it also specifically adjures the working-class parties – the German Communists in particular – never to cease for a single instant 'to instil into the working class the clearest possible recognition of the hostile antagonism between bourgeoisie and proletariat'.[15] A similar message is implicit in *Capital* and some of Engels's later writings; but the specific role of that 'material force' of which Marx had written – the role of ideology in class struggle – was never systematically spelled out. It was inevitable, therefore, that the question should arise, and be dealt with in a more or less theoretical way in the Social Democratic parties that arose in Western Europe towards the end of Marx's life. Even in England, where Marxist theory has had little influence in the labour movement, William Morris reflected in the early 1890s that the working people had ceased to desire real socialism and argued that a socialist party's most vital task was to foster a real socialist consciousness among working people, so that they should 'understand themselves to be face to face with false society, themselves the only possible elements of true society'.[16] But, at the time, his was a small voice crying in the wilderness.

The situation was a rather different one in Russia when Lenin, almost on the eve of the revolution of 1905, concerned himself with the creation of a party of 'a new type', one trained in Marxist principles and also able to convey them to the industrial workers, recently arrived from the villages, who were now engaged in the first bitter economic engagements with their employers. But far from believing that the workers' militancy, focused on economic targets, would automatically and spontaneously engender in them a political consciousness of class, Lenin denounced those who believed it and stated roundly that 'class political consciousness can be brought to the workers only *from without,* that is, only from outside the economic struggle, from outside the sphere of relations between workers and employers'; and he added that 'all worship of the spontaneity of the labour movement, all belittling of the role of the "conscious element", of the role of the party of Social Democracy, means . . . *strengthening the influence of . . . bourgeois ideology* among the workers'. In short, 'the only choice is: either the BOURGEOIS or the SOCIALIST ideology. There is no middle course. . . . Hence to belittle the socialist ideology in any way . . . means to strengthen the bourgeois ideology.'[17] Élitism? no doubt. But it must be remembered that, under the conditions then prevailing, Lenin did not believe that the time had yet come for the creation of a mass party able to *learn* from, as well as able to teach the masses.

The Russian Revolution followed; and, after the first enthusiasms and the defeat of the revolution in the West, speculation about revolution and a working-class revolutionary ideology took a more philosophical turn.[18] Among the most illustrious of the Marxist intellectuals in the West who returned to the question of revolutionary ideology were the Hungarian Georg Lukács and the Italian Antonio Gramsci. Lukács wrote a book on the subject: his *History and Class Consciousness* was published in 1922. Lukács went back to Hegel and borrowed from him the notion that to arrive at *total truth* Subject and Object – by nature antithetical – had to become fully merged and identified. Hegel had seen this possibility in the case of art, religion and what he called the realm of the Absolute Spirit; but, hampered by his notion of mind as history's 'universal agent', he saw no way to affect this reconciliation in the case of history. So, with Hegel, it remained an abstraction. Lukács attempted to overcome Hegel's dilemma by following Marx's example in 'turning' him 'upside down' and taking over from Marx his twin notions of class consciousness and 'false reality' and applying them to society. 'Total truth', he argued against Hegel, could only be attained through class struggle for total hegemony. But no class, he considered, was capable of arriving at 'total truth', that is at an awareness of reality, until industrialization made this possible by polarizing society into two opposing classes, bourgeoisie and proletariat. But the bourgeoisie could not reconcile its class interests with any serious attempt to dispel the fantasies of 'false reality'; and, in consequence, the proletariat, as the most 'alienated' class and, therefore, the most anxious to transform itself in the process of achieving a new hegemony, could attain this 'true' knowledge or awareness. And from Marx he also learned to see consciousness not as a form of intellectual exercise but as the close ally of 'practical critical activity' (or *praxis*), whose aim it was to change the world. This again was strictly at variance with Hegel's purely élitist notion of an Absolute Spirit counterposed against the ignorant mass.

But the proletariat, as with Marx, could only attain this 'ultimate goal' as the result of a protracted struggle; for long this aim could only be a 'mission' or something potential to the class. (At this stage of his argument, he quotes Marx's passage on *'what the proletariat is'* that we noted above.)[19] But, meanwhile, the proletarians are groping in the dark, victims of the "false consciousness' imposed on them, in Lukács's totally polarized society, by the bourgeoisie. One form that this 'falsity' of vision takes is the separation that is made between the economic and political battles; and here, of course, he falls back on the argument used by Lenin against the 'Economists' in 1902. 'The most striking division,' he writes, 'in proletarian class consciousness and that most fraught with consequences is the separation of the economic struggle from the political one.'[20]

So far so good; but there are two serious obstacles to using Lukács as a safe guide to the understanding of working-class struggle, let alone of the struggles of other protesting groups.

One is that the society he envisages is totally polarized between the two major classes in industrial society; the peasants are treated as a virtual anachronism from the past and such intermediate groups as shopkeepers or artisans count for nothing (a strange vista to choose for one sprung from an agrarian and industrially undeveloped country like Hungary on the morrow of the First World War). And, secondly, how is the proletariat expected to arrive at its 'total' awareness as a prelude to taking over state power? By struggle in the first place – but not 'by isolated skirmishes'. In theory, therefore, Lukács follows Marx and Lenin; but, in fact, he depends far more for a working-class awakening on the prospect of the inevitable crisis of capitalism. Thus, in practice, the proletariat is left to stand on the side-lines as silent spectators while capitalism digs its grave. This, of course, considerably limits the value of Lukács as a guide to the ideology of popular protest.[21]

This brings us to Gramsci, who, like Lukács, lived through the crisis of military defeat and revolution that attended the end and aftermath of the First World War, but whose experience as an active militant and as a ten-year prisoner of Fascism was to be very different from his. In his *Prison Notebooks*, written in jail but only published a generation later, Gramsci takes us far nearer than even Marx and Lenin – let alone Lukács – to a theory of popular, as well as working-class, ideology of protest. Admittedly, in order to evade the censor, Gramsci's language is often obscure and his ideas, widely scattered over a disordered text, easily lead to confusion. Yet the originality of his views on ideology is clear enough. He distinguishes between 'historically organic ideologies; those, that is, which are necessary to a given structure, and ideologies that are arbitrary, rationalistic, or "willed"'. The first of these, which concern him most, 'have a validity which is "psychological", they "organize" human masses, and create the terrain on which men move, acquire consciousness of their positive struggle, etc.'[22] Such being his interest, he virtually ignores the old Marxist notion of 'false consciousness' which plays such a vital part in Lukács' system. It is also natural, therefore, that ideology, while anchored (like other elements in the 'superstructure') to the material base, should be seen as playing a relatively independent role as that would-be 'material force' of which Marx had written. But to

Gramsci ideology becomes more 'liberated' still, as it ceases to be the exclusive preserve of what he terms the 'fundamental classes' in industrial society; there is room in his system, too, for those less structured forms of thought that circulate among the common people, often contradictory and confused and compounded of folklore, myth and day-to-day popular experience; these count among what he calls 'non-organic' ideology. This already opens the door to the study of alternative 'middle' or 'lower-class' modes of thought which Marxism, at least in relation to modern society, has tended to ignore. Not only does this bring peasants and artisans back into the picture, but it provides the working class with allies which a purely polarized society, like that conceived by Lukács, would necessarily exclude.

But Gramsci's main contribution to the social study of ideas is the use he makes of the phenomenon of 'hegemony'. To Gramsci hegemony is no longer merely a system of domination, whether of ideas or political power. It is rather the process than the system that concerns him – the process whereby the ruling class imposes a consensus, its dominion in the realm of ideas, by largely peaceful means. This happens through its control of the media of indoctrination in that part of the state that he terms 'civil society': through press, church and education. Thus the people become willing partners in their own subjection. How, then, can the proletariat, representing the majority, shake off this ideological servitude? Only, says Gramsci, by building up a counter-ideology of its own as an antidote to that of the ruling class and as an essential preliminary to its capture of control of the state. But it must have its own trained agents, as the bourgeoisie had theirs, to establish its hegemony; these are the 'organic' intellectuals (Gramsci uses this term for the professional agents of both 'fundamental' classes). The aim of the 'organic' intellectuals working in the interests of the proletariat must be not only to equip their own class with the new ideology – the ideology of 'praxis' (Gramsci's code-name for Marxism) – but to win over or neutralize and detach from their former allegiance what he calls the 'traditional' intellectuals, who, reflecting the interests of 'traditional' classes like peasants and craftsmen, are not deeply committed to either 'fundamental' class. In this way, according to Gramsci, the proletariat may both build its own counter-ideology and weaken the ideological defences of its opponents before defeating them in the struggle for state power.

The implications of Gramsci's writing are, of course, of considerable importance for anyone writing a book like this. He abandons the crude division of ideology (consciousness) into 'true' and 'false' and bridges the yawning chasm that Lukács and others have created between the Elect and the non-Elect, which allows for no historical progression from the one to the other. Gramsci's approach is more historical; he is concerned with growth and development, as shown in his notion of the gradual building of a counter-ideology to destroy the ruling class's hegemony and in his recognition of surviving 'traditional' classes which, even when society is largely divided between the two 'fundamental' classes, have an important role to play. Following Marx and Engels, he also stresses the importance of studying each historical situation afresh and in depth, including the ideology appropriate to the occasion. ('"Ideology" itself must be analysed historically, in the terms of the philosophy of praxis, as a superstructure.')[23] So the ground is prepared for the study of popular ideology over a wider field: not only among the proletarians of industrial society, but among their forebears, the peasants, smallholders and small townsmen of a transitional society, when the 'fundamental' classes of today were still in the process of formation.

Author's Note

It may be objected that, in this chapter, I have been unduly selective, concentrating on a half-dozen Marxist writers and neglecting men who, whether Marxists or not, have made important contributions to the study of ideology in the course of the past century. This would be true enough if they could be shown to have made contributions not only to the theory of ideology but (in accordance with the subject of this book) to that aspect of ideology which relates to the protest of common people, both proletarians and others. To mention a few of the most distinguished of those who have written in the half-century since the First World War: among the non-Marxists, the two outstanding theorists whose works have been translated into

English are Karl Mannheim and Max Weber. In his *Protestant Ethic and the Spirit of Capitalism* (London, 1930), Weber accepts Marx's proposition that 'the ideas of the ruling class are in every epoch the ruling ideas'; and he illustrates this acceptance in his presentation of symbols as 'legitimations' of class domination. Yet, in general, he rejects Marx's theory of class and opposes the notion that capitalism generates its own capitalist ideology, while stressing that Puritan ideas were a useful tool in the development of capitalism with which it has a 'spiritual' affinity. But 'popular' ideology plays no part in this scheme. This is true to a lesser degree of Karl Mannheim's *Ideology and Utopia* (Routledge, 1936), in which the notion of 'Utopia', as a counter to 'Ideology', is presented as often reflecting the political thinking of 'certain oppressed groups' desirous of affecting 'a transformation of existing society'. But that is as far as it goes.

Among more recent non-Marxists, mention may be made of C. Geertz, 'Ideology as a Cultural System', in *Ideology and Discontent*, ed. D. E. Apter (1964) pp. 47–76; George Lichtheim, *The Concept of Ideology and other Essays* (1967); John Plamenatz, *Ideology* (Praeger, n.d.); and (in parts) C. Wright Mills, *The Sociological Imagination* (1959), esp. pp. 8–9, 36–7; but these, too, are not concerned with ideology in relation to popular protest. The same is equally true of two eminent Marxist scholars writing on ideology and related subjects today: Louis Althusser and Lucio Colletti. Althusser has made valuable additions to Marxist theory, giving it a historical perspective that it has often lacked (as in *Lenin and Philosophy and other Essays* (1971) and *Politics and History* (1972)); yet his 'structuralist' method is too inflexible to make him a useful guide to historical enquiry. Colletti has been mainly concerned – as in *From Rousseau to Lenin* (1972) – to reinterpret Marx and, *int. al.*, to defend Marxism against the 'romanticism' of Herbert Marcuse. But he, too, has not been concerned with such problems as arise in the following chapters.

NOTES

1. G. Lichtheim, *The Concept of Ideology and Other Essays*, New York, 1967, pp. 4–11.
2. ibid., pp. 11–17.

The Ideology of Popular Protest

Our first chapter was mainly concerned with the Marxist theory of the ideology of working-class protest, or its challenge to capitalist class rule in modern industrial society. We saw that, with the exception of Gramsci's notion of the 'traditional' classes, this left little room for the struggles of peasants and urban shopkeepers and artisans, whether in present-day society or in the 'pre-industrial' society that spanned the transition between a feudal and a capitalist mode of production. So a theory of ideology designed to meet another purpose – to define the struggle between the two major contending classes in modern industrial society – will obviously be irrelevant here; and as it is with this transitional society and with these 'traditional' social groups – as yet not evolved into identifiable social classes – that we shall be largely concerned in the following chapters, we shall have to find a new theory or 'model' of the ideology of protest, one suited to the 'popular' movements of the times.

Earlier writers have noted the difference between two types of ideology, applicable to those times as well as to our own: the difference between a structured, or relatively structured, type of ideology (the only 'ideology' to be worthy of the name, according to some)[1] and one of more simple attitudes, *mentalités* or outlooks.[2] To limit ourselves to the first of these would not take us far in a study of 'popular' ideology; and the second, while more appropriate in a study such as this, is quite inadequate in itself. Equally, we must discard such notions as that underlying Oscar Lewis's theory of a 'culture of poverty' for, as its title suggests, it is concerned with passivity and acceptance;[3] and though the notion of 'class' enters into it (in the sense of an awareness of social inferiority in the relations between 'them' and 'us')[4] it could have little contribution to make to a discussion of the ideology of popular protest. Even Althusser's statement that 'there is no practice except by and in ideology' (which is fair enough as far as it goes)[5] does not take us far. So we shall have to substitute for all these a theory of our own.

Popular ideology in this period is not a purely internal affair and the sole property of a single class or group: that in itself distinguishes it from ideology as 'class consciousness' or its antithesis, as we saw it treated in the previous chapter. It is most often a mixture, a fusion of two elements, of which only one is the peculiar property of the 'popular' classes and the other is superimposed by a process of transmission and adoption from outside. Of these, the first is what I call the 'inherent', traditional element – a sort of 'mother's milk' ideology, based on direct experience, oral tradition or folk-memory and not learned by listening to sermons or speeches or reading books. In this fusion the second element is the stock of ideas and beliefs that are 'derived' or borrowed from others, often taking the form of a more structured system of ideas, political or religious, such as the Rights of Man, Popular Sovereignty, *Laissez-faire* and the Sacred Right of Property, Nationalism, Socialism, or the various versions of justification by Faith. So two things are important to note: one is that there is no such thing as a *tabula rasa*, or an empty tablet in the place of a mind on which new ideas may be grafted where there were no ideas before (a notion dear to the proponents of the 'mindless rabble'); and the second is that there is also no such thing as an automatic progression from 'simple' to more sophisticated ideas. (It will be remembered that Lenin most vigorously denied the possibility of a spontaneous generation of such ideas among the Russian workers in 1902.) But it is equally important to realize – and this is closely related to what has just been said – that there is no Wall of Babylon dividing the two types of ideology, so that one cannot simply describe the second as being 'superior' or at a higher level than the first. There is, in fact, a considerable overlap between them. For instance, among the 'inherent' beliefs of one generation, and forming part of its basic culture, are many beliefs that were originally derived from outside by an earlier one.

An example of this is the notion of the 'Norman Yoke', of which Christopher Hill has written.[6] This notion ultimately goes back to the ancient 'liberties' filched from the 'freedom-loving English' by William the Norman (sometimes inelegantly termed the Bastard) and his Norman Knights or Banditti, and which, enriched by later experience, became an important popular legend that did service to the popular movement in England up to the time of Chartism in the 1830s and 1840s.

The same is true of religious ideas, such as those embodied in the teachings of Luther and Calvin which, once they had been coopted by the Protestant State and thundered from the pulpit by generations of Protestant preachers and divines, had, by the seventeenth century, in one form or another become part of the 'inherent' ideology or culture of the people at large. Again, the second type, the 'derived' ideology, can only be effectively absorbed if the ground has already been well prepared; otherwise, it will be rejected as surely as the Spanish peasants of 1794 rejected the doctrine of the Rights of Man (when Germans and Italians, and even Catholic Poles and Irish, had welcomed it) or as African peoples or Pacific Islanders today, recently evolved from a tribal or feudal society, find it hard to accommodate themselves to the blessings of *laissez-faire*. And, of course, this type of ideological resistance is not peculiar to the common people, whether in Africa, New Guinea or anywhere else. Felix Raab, an Australian, has written of the different receptions given by successive generations of sixteenth and seventeenth-century English gentry and people at Court to the radical ideas of Machiavelli: what was anathema to one generation was acceptable to the next and just a yawn to the third.[7]

But it is not only a question of receptivity; it is perhaps even more significant that the derived or more 'structured' ideas are often a more sophisticated distillation of popular experience and the people's 'inherent' beliefs. So, in fact, there is no one-way traffic but constant interaction between the two. Marx himself, possibly the greatest purveyor of 'derived' ideas in history, wrote in the *Manifesto* that 'they (the Communists) merely express, in general terms, actual relations springing from an existing class struggle . . . from a historical movement going on under our very eyes'.[8] Looking back on Marx's work as a whole, Althusser, the French Communist philosopher, elaborates on this idea: 'Without the proletariat's class struggle, Marx could not have adopted the point of view of class exploitation, or carried out his scientific work. In this scientific work, which bears the mark of all his culture and genius, *he has given back to the workers' movement in a theoretical form what he took from it in a political and ideological form.*'⁹ Nor is this peculiar to Marx: it is impossible not to see a link between Rousseau's democratic ideas and the battle for democracy being waged in his native Geneva long before it was waged anywhere else in Europe, let alone beyond it; and a young American scholar suggests in a recent book review that the experience – and 'inherent' ideology – of the silk-weavers of Lyon, the first workers in France to fight *politically* for the right of 'association' (this was in the early 1830s), may have contributed to the formulation of the cooperative theories of the French socialist thinkers, Proudhon and Louis Blanc, who wrote a few years later.¹⁰

But where, then, more exactly, should one draw the line between the two ideologies? By 'inherent' beliefs I mean, for one thing, the peasant's belief in his right to land, whether owned individually or in common ownership with others. It is a belief that informs the protests of the Mexican or Colombian or New Guinean peasants today as it informed those of the European peasants in their great rebellions of 1381, 1525 and 1789, the risings against tax-collectors in Tokugawa Japan, the land-hunger of the Irish through the greater part of the nineteenth century, or the Englishman's resistance to enclosure between the sixteenth and eighteenth centuries. Analogous to the peasant's belief in the common justice of being allowed unfettered possession of his land is the belief of the small consumer, whether a villager or townsman, in his right to buy bread at a 'just' price, as determined by experience and custom,¹¹ or the worker's claim to a 'just' wage and not simply one that responds to the whim of his employer or to the new-fangled notion of supply and demand. The proliferation of food riots in the eighteenth and early nineteenth centuries in France and England and the battles of the Luddites and machine-breaking labourers in the southern counties of England in the post-Napoleonic period bear eloquent testimony to the persistence of these demands.

Similarly, the 'free-born' Englishman of those times invoked his traditional 'liberties' and rioted if he was denied them, and the small freeholder and townsman resisted the attempts of 'improving' landlords and farmers, enterprising bourgeois or civic authorities (just as many do still today) to uproot them or disrupt their traditional communities in the name of progress. Such people tended to prefer the 'devil they knew' to the one they did not and to be 'backward' rather than 'forward'-looking in the sense that they were more inclined to demand the restoration of rights that were lost or were threatened with expropriation than change or reform. But there were others – and not only among 'primitive rebels' or primitive societies – who held millenarial or chiliastic beliefs and were, therefore, more inclined to stake their fortunes on a sudden change or regeneration, such as that promised by a Second Coming of Christ or the more mundane 'good news' of Louis XVI's decision to summon the Estates General to meet in the summer of 1789.[12]

There are also the less tangible – less easily documented – aspects, such as what French writers like Leroy Ladurie, Mandrou and Vovelle have called the *mentalités* and *sensibilité collective* of the common people, which, like the varying elements in E. P. Thompson's 'plebeian culture', are by no means confined to protest. Yet they may have their importance in this respect as well and Michel Vovelle has shown us how the *sensibilité collective* of French peasants and urban *menu peuple* in some ways – such as in their changed attitudes to religion and death and their behaviour in popular festivals at the end of the Old Regime – anticipated certain aspects of popular ideology displayed in the revolutionary *journées* of 1789.[13]

This type of ideology may take the form of a mixture of often disparate beliefs, among which it is hard to tell the truly 'inherent' element from that more recently 'derived'; this corresponds broadly to what Gramsci meant by the 'contradictory' element in the ideology of the Italian common people. Hobsbawm cites the case of the Italian brigand leader of the 1860s – at the time of Garibaldi's wars – who issued a proclamation that ran:

> Out with the traitors, out with the beggars, long live the fair kingdom of Naples with its most religious sovereign, long live the vicar of Christ, Pius IX, and long live our ardent republican brothers.[14]

At a lower social level, the Irish peasant Defenders of the 1780s had an even more confused ideology, in which nationalism, republican and Catholic sentiments and devotion to the American and French revolutions all jockeyed for position.[15]

A similar medley of loyalties (though, in this case, it is hardly confusion) lies in the continued devotion to King, Tsar or Emperor among peasants who are up in arms against the landlords or the royal government itself; this was particularly evident in Europe during the period of Autocracy or Absolute Monarchy. In France, before the Revolution, new monarchs were greeted with displays of genuine popular enthusiasm and rioting peasants displayed their loyalty in such double-edged slogans as 'Vive le Roi et sans gabelle' (as in 1674), or 'Vive le Roi et que le pain ramende!' (as in 1775); and it took over two years of revolution and nine months of 'revolutionary' war before even the citizens of Paris (let alone the peasants) were ready to see the King executed for treason. And from Russia, in the following century, Hobsbawm cites two telling examples of the peasants' continuing loyalty to the Tsar, their Protector, long after they have seen cause to hate or distrust his ministers. The first is from the Volga at the time of Alexander II, when rebellious peasants accost the general sent to suppress them in the following terms: 'Don't fire on us, you are shooting on Alexander Nikoleyevitch, you are shedding the blood of the Tsar.'[16] The second is from Poltava in 1902, when peasants pillaging an estate are reminded by a threatened landlord that he has always been their friend. 'But what are we to do?', several voices answered him. 'We aren't doing this in our name, but in the name of the Tsar.'[17]

But how far can this 'inherent' ideology by itself carry the protesters? Into strikes, food riots, peasant rebellions (with or without success); and even into a state of awareness of the need for radical change (what French historians call a 'prise de conscience'); but evidently it cannot bring them all the way to revolution, even as junior partners of the bourgeoisie. The limits are suggested by E. P. Thompson when he explains how a plebeian culture in eighteenth-century England – the 'self-activating culture of the people derived from their own experience and resources' – was able, in several respects, to prevent the hegemony of the gentry from becoming all-

pervasive. Among popular achievements in the course of this
resistance he instances: the maintenance of their traditional
culture; the partial arrest of the work-discipline of early
industrialism; the enlargement of the scope of the Poor Laws;
the assurance of more plentiful supplies of grain; and, in
addition, 'they enjoyed liberties of pushing about the streets
and jostling, gaping and huzzaing, pulling down the houses of
obnoxious bakers or Dissenters, and a generally riotous
disposition which astonished foreign visitors, and which almost
led them into believing that they were "free"'.[18]

But similar popular achievements, whether in 'pre-industrial'
England or elsewhere, could not advance far beyond this point
without the native 'plebeian culture' or 'inherent' ideology
becoming supplemented by that 'derived' element of which I
spoke before: the political, philosophical or religious ideas
that, at varying stages of sophistication, became absorbed in
the more specifically *popular* culture. These, in the historical
context of which I am speaking, tended to be 'forward' rather
than 'backward'-looking, positing reform rather than
restoration, and were more often than not – again, in the period
of what Robert Palmer has called the 'Democratic Revolution' –
those transmitted, sometimes at second remove, by the main
challengers to aristocracy, the up-and-coming bourgeoisie. But
they might be conservative or 'backward'-looking, as in the
'Church-and-King' movements of French peasants in the
Vendée after 1793, of Neapolitan and Roman citizens against
the French in 1798–9, or of Spanish peasants against Napoleon
in 1808: yet, in the first of these examples, it is interesting to note
that the Vendéan peasants went through the revolutionary
process first and only turned against the Jacobin Convention in
Paris when the Revolution appeared to be running directly
counter to their hopes.

In either case, this indoctrination – or, more accurately, this
merger of 'inherent' and 'derived' ideas – took place in stages
and at different levels of sophistication. At the most elementary
stage, it might take the form of slogans, like the Americans'
'Death to revenue officers' and 'No taxation without
representation'; or the 'No Excise' or 'No Popery' shouted by
eighteenth-century Londoners; or, again, the 'Vive le
Parlement' and shortly after the 'Vive le tiers état' chanted by the

Parisian *menu peuple* on the eve of revolution. As a variant, there was the use of symbols like 'Popery and wooden shoes' or the ritual planting of Liberty Trees and the conversion of the traditional Pope-burning into the burning in effigy of George III's ministers in pre-Revolution Boston. At a slightly higher level of sophistication came the incorporation into popular speech of such radical terms as 'patriots' (this applied to all three countries), and (in France) 'social contract', 'Third Estate' and the 'Rights of Man'. The latter also gave its name to the more structured political programme of revolution in the Declaration of Rights in France (August 1789) which followed the earlier programme of revolution in America proclaimed in the Declaration of Independence of 1776.

The means whereby these new ideas were transmitted naturally varied between one country and another; but, in all, of course, a great deal depended on the state of literacy among the common people. Accurate statistics are hard to come by and such literacy tests as were made, signatures on marriage registers, on police reports and the like, varied from country to country and even from region to region. But with the help of such tests as scholars have interpreted for us, we may surmise that, on the eve of the eighteenth-century 'age of revolutions', the American *menu peuple*, being more versed in Bible-reading, were probably more literate than the English and the English (having by now, like the Americans, virtually no peasantry) more literate than the French. Rough calculations suggest that, of the larger cities (and America had none large enough to rate as such) Paris and London may have had a popular literacy rate of about 40–50 per cent – with labourers trailing behind craftsmen and women well behind the two.[19] So perhaps rather less than one half of the Parisian *menu peuple*, and six or seven in ten of the craftsmen, could sign their names or read the revolutionary message of the day purveyed by the numerous tracts and simply-written journals of the day. (Rousseau's writings were for a literacy élite only and were only likely to reach the plebeian reader at second or third remove.) But even the written word could be conveyed by other means: in the French provinces of 1789, for example, passages from journals and letters relating to the great events taking place at Versailles and Paris were read aloud from the balcony of the *hôtel de ville* in cities and market towns. But even more pervasive was the spoken word whose transmission might be made through the pulpit, the army or meetings of the Puritan elect (as in England in the 1640s); whereas in France in 1789, it was in the small workshop, the typical unit of industrial production in the city at that time, that the craftsman acquired from his master the slogans and discussed together the great events in the new idiom of the day. In Paris, in addition, there were the wine shops, markets and baker's shops, which for both men and women served both as a forum for debate and as launching pads for popular agitation and revolt.

So, by one means or another, these 'derived' notions became grafted onto the 'inherent' notions and beliefs and the new popular ideology took shape as an amalgam of the two. This process, not surprisingly, took place more quickly in towns than in villages and far more quickly in times of revolution (from which most of my examples have been drawn) than in times of social and political calm. But, it must be emphasized, whether the resultant mixture took on a militant and revolutionary or a conservative and counter-revolutionary form depended less on the nature of the recipients or of the 'inherent' beliefs from which they started than on the nature of the 'derived' beliefs compounded by the circumstances then prevailing and what E. P. Thompson has called 'the sharp jostle of experience'.[20] What I am arguing is that there are three factors and not only two to be taken account of: the 'inherent' element which, as we noted before, was the common base; the 'derived', or outside, element, which could only be effectively absorbed if the ground was already prepared; and the circumstances and experience which, in the final analysis, determined the nature of the final mixture. In this way only can we understand why the *sans-culottes* of Paris remained revolutionary while many of their confrères at Lyon, Marseille and other cities, whose 'inherent' beliefs were broadly the same as their own and who had experienced a similar baptism of revolution, later, under the impact of a new set of ('Girondin') ideas, changed their allegiance; and why the Vendée peasants, with similar 'inherent' beliefs and aspirations to peasants in the rest of France, in the conditions prevailing in the spring of 1793, allowed their former revolutionary ideas to be pushed aside by others.

However, it is not quite so simple; for, in all such cases and however 'the cookie (eventually) crumbles', the stubbornness of the original 'inherent' beliefs are such that the new 'derived' ideas, whether progressive or conservative, that come through the channels of transmission – and this is not peculiar to the 'pre-industrial' period – are not likely to be the same as those that went in. So the process of grafting was never a simple A + B affair. Had the 'inherent' element been a purely passive recipient then perhaps it might. But, in fact, in the case of all classes, and not of the 'popular' classes alone, all 'derived' ideas in the course of transmission and adoption suffer a transformation or 'sea-change': its nature will depend on the social needs or the political aims of the classes that are ready to absorb them. It was a lesson that Martin Luther learned in the 1520s, when the German peasants, much to his indignation, took his teachings at their face value and used them to sustain their rebellion against the princes, who to Luther were benefactors and not, as they were to the peasants, oppressors. The French bourgeoisie, finding themselves in the late 1780s with the need to make a revolution, picked on Rousseau's theory of 'popular sovereignty' and his 'social contract' to provide an ideological justification for their rebellion against nobility and royal despotism; this was long after the French aristocratic Parlement and the aristocrats of Hungary and Poland had begun to make a very different use of Rousseau's ideas – as well as Montesquieu's – in order to bolster the 'aristocratic element' against the Crown. The French 'lower orders' – in particular, the *sans-culottes* in Paris – learned their lesson and, having acquired the new idiom of revolution from the liberal aristocracy and bourgeoisie, adapted it in turn to their own uses and, on occasion, turned it to good account against their former teachers. We shall hear more of this in a later chapter.

A final question – that we shall only touch on here – is what happens to this new popular ideology, forged in the fire of revolution, when the 'popular' phase of the revolution is over or when the counter-revolution sets in? Does it mean, for instance, that after the defeat of the English Levellers at Burford in 1649, of the Parisian *sans-culottes* in 1795, or for that matter of the French *ouvriers* in June 1848 – does it mean that all the political experience they had gained in the course of revolution was lost and would have to start again when the next round of revolutions followed after a suitable respite? No, obviously not. The reaction might be real enough, as it was under the Cromwellian Protectorate and Restoration in England and the Napoleonic Empire and Restoration in France. But what is also true is that the popular revolutionary tradition, having led an underground existence out of sight of the authorities, survived and re-emerged in new forms and under new historical conditions when the 'people' – the recipients of the previous set of 'derived' ideas – had also suffered a 'sea-change'. But this, too, will be discussed further in later chapters.

NOTES

1. e.g. Karl Mannheim and Cornelius Geertz (see p. 25 above).
2. See John Plamenatz's definition of ideology as 'a set of closely related beliefs, or ideas, or even attitudes, characteristic of a group or community' (*Ideology*, op. cit., p. 15). For ideology as *mentalité*, see various passages in E. Leroy Ladurie, R. Mandrou and M. Vovelle; also p. 31 and n. 13 below.
3. O. Lewis, 'The Culture of Poverty', *Scientific American*, CCXI (1966), pp. 19–25.
4. Richard Hoggart makes a somewhat similar distinction when describing modern working-class attitudes; see his chapter on 'Them' and 'Us' in *The Uses of Literacy* (London, 1957), pp. 72–101.
5. *Lenin and Philosophy* . . ., p. 170.
6. C. Hill, 'The Norman Yoke', in *Democracy and the Labour Movement*, ed. John Saville, London, 1954, pp. 11–66.
7. Felix Raab, *The English Face of Machiavelli*, London, 1964.
8. *Communist Manifesto*, op. cit., p. 50.
9. *Lenin and Philosophy*, op. cit., p. 9 (my italics).
10. William H. Sewell, in reviewing Robert Bezucha's *The Lyon Uprising of 1834* . . . in *Social History*, 5: May 1977, pp. 688–9. This is not a perfect example, as the basic ideas of the Lyonnais workers and small masters had already been somewhat diluted and 'politicized' by their recent association (in 1834 but not in 1831) with the Young Republicans of the city.
11. See, especially, E. P. Thompson, 'The Moral Economy of the English Crowd of the Eighteenth Century', *Past and Present*, no. 50, May 1971, pp. 76–136.
12. See also the short-lived millenarial movement of Kentish farm labourers in 1838, in P. G. Rogers, *Battle in Bossenden Wood*, London, 1961.
13. M. Vovelle, 'Le tournant des mentalités en France 1750–1789: la "sensibilité" pré-révolutionnaire', *Social History*, 5, May 1977, pp. 605–29.
14. E. J. Hobsbawm, *Primitive Rebels* (Manchester, 1959), p. 29.

15. See a Defender's catechism quoted by M. R. Beames, *Journal of Peasant Studies*, July 1975, p. 504. For similar confusion in the ideology of cargo cults and strike movements in modern times in New Guinea, see E. Ogan, 'Cargoism and Politics in Bougainville 1962–1972', *Journal of Pacific History*, ix (1974), pp. 117–29; and B. Gammage, 'The Rabaul Strike, 1929', ibid., x (1975), pp. 3–29.

16. *Primitive Rebels*, p. 121.

17. ibid., p. 186.

18. E. P. Thompson, 'Eighteenth-Century English Society: Class struggle without class?', *Social History*, iii (2), May 1978, 137–65, esp. 164–5.

19. For a discussion of popular literacy in eighteenth-century France, see D. Mornet, *Les origines intellectuelles de la Révolution française*, Paris 1933, pp. 420–5; and (for Paris) G. Rudé, *The Crowd in the French Revolution*, Oxford, 1959, pp. 210–11. For eighteenth-century Britain, see a number of articles in *Past and Present*, esp. Lawrence Stone, 'Literacy and Education in England, 1640–1900', no. 42, February 1969, pp. 69–139; and Michael Sanderson, 'Literacy and Social Mobility in the Industrial Revolution in England', no. 56, August 1972, pp. 75–104. Both show a relatively high literacy rate for labourers and servants (about 40 per cent) around 1700–1750 and a sharp decline in the third quarter, rising again briefly around 1775. But there are no reliable national figures for Britain before 1840.

20. The full sentence runs: 'This culture (the 'self-activating plebeian culture'] . . . constitutes an ever-present threat to official descriptions of reality; given the sharp jostle of experience, the intrusion of "seditious" propagandists, the Church-and-King crowd can become Jacobin or Luddite, the loyal Tsarist navy can become an insurrectionary Bolshevik fleet.' Thompson, op. cit., p. 164. Which is more or less what I am saying, too. But I am also arguing that the process may be reversed or, at least, take another turn: the 'Bolshevik fleet' also had its 'Kronstadt'. Or, again, as we shall see, the class-conscious worker of Oldham (1830s-style) may become an advocate of class collaboration before 1848 (see pp. 154, 158 below).

Part Two

PEASANTS

1

In Medieval Europe

First, to consider the case of peasants, beginning with Europe in the Middle Ages. The typical peasant of medieval Europe was a petty rural cultivator living on his land, who worked both for his lord and for himself, and whose economy – whether he cultivated crops of olives or wines in the warm dry climate of the Mediterranean or grew wheat or (later) potatoes or reared sheep or cattle in the plains and valleys of the more humid and intemperate East and West – was essentially self-sufficient; and it is remarkable, as Rodney Hilton explains, how little money the medieval peasant householder had to spend on luxuries or on urban commodities for himself and his family even at a time when medieval civilization was at its peak.[1]

The main reason for this situation lay not so much in the dearth of skills or techniques or in the poverty of the soil that the peasant was called on to cultivate, as in the relationships established from about the tenth century on between the small cultivator, whose labour lay at the basis of all wealth, and the landed magnate or lesser nobleman who, directly or indirectly, owned the greater part of the land and had reduced the peasant to bondage. Under this 'feudal' system the lords were bound to the King or the Duke by personal vassalage and, in return for leading his armies or levies, were given land (defined as 'military' tenures) and control and jurisdiction over the mass of the peasantry. Thus the peasant became a villein or a serf, tied to the land and, even if not actually bound to the soil by law, compelled by contract to work so many days in the year on the lord's demesne and to render a multiplicity of other services in cash or kind that left him little surplus or opportunity to develop his own land, or to make the best economic use of his right to graze and glean or gather wood in the common field or forest. The original justification for this human bondage was that the lord was thereby rewarded for the protection he gave the peasants in his seigneurial court of justice. This may have made some sense in the 'Dark Ages' of early feudalism, when traditional justice had broken down and the emerging medieval monarchies were wracked by baronial brigandage and civil war; but it had certainly ceased to serve this purpose by the eleventh century in Western and Southern Europe, as the seigneurial courts and levies had by then already developed into the means for coercing and exploiting the peasant in the lord's interest rather than of affording him protection against lawless bands of brigands.

If personal servitude was the main feature of medieval feudalism in Western Europe (in the East, for reasons that will be suggested in a later chapter, serfdom only reached its zenith in the eighteenth century), its operation was by no means universal. While the precept 'nulle terre sans seigneur' might be fairly generally observed, there were small pockets of free peasants in parts of Germany and Scandinavia (and fairly generally in northern Italy) who enjoyed the status of free men (and some remained so even at the height of the feudal reaction that extended serfdom in the fourteenth century and later) unbound to either soil or *seigneur*; and there were many more who, though formally tied to the lord's demesne, were still practically unfree in the sense that they had to pay the traditional rent for the use of their land, to carry their corn to the lord's mill to be ground, pay fines (or heriots) when sons or daughters married or when any part of their properties changed hands (known in France as *lods et ventes*), or to pay other numerous dues or taxes that varied from one demesne or region to another. Moreover, the lords enjoyed further privileges in the purchase or sale of grain and in hunting and fishing rights and access to common pastures; and similar privileges and forms of bondage were by no means peculiar to Medieval Europe, as will be seen in later chapters.

Under these circumstances, it is not surprising that peasant demands and protests should centre on the redress of grievances relating to serfdom, to the alleviation of onerous services and dues, and freedom from the oppressive monopolies enjoyed by the nobility and gentry. But, Hilton tells us, the demand for land or the confiscation of large estates (familiar to modern peasant movements) was rarely voiced by rebellious peasants in the Middle Ages, particularly where arable land was concerned; and he adds that the medieval equivalent to the later demand for confiscation took the form of demands for lower rents and less onerous services or for the abolition of the more obnoxious of the monopolies usurped by the lords.[2]

Though peasant rebellions tended to cluster around the later Middle Ages when the old feudal system, based on vassalage and serfdom, in Western Europe was in the process of dissolution, there were cases of violent peasant protest going back almost to the 'salad days' of feudalism in prosperous regions like Normandy or northern Italy. Examples are recorded of the forcible assertion of the right to fish and hunt by Norman peasants against their Duke in 996; and, between 882 and 905, of a dispute between peasants on Lake Como and their lord, the abbey of St Ambrose, Milan, over the services exacted. And, as often happened, these initial demands were followed by others that went nearer to the heart of the matter, to the existence of serfdom itself. These wider implications were also sometimes touched upon (though they were seldom officially recorded) in statements attributed to the peasants themselves. Thus we learn that the rebellious Norman peasants of 996 were heard to say, 'nus sumes homes come il le sunt' and that, in a dispute over villein services in late thirteenth-century England, peasants actually cried 'nulli servire volumus'.[4] (It is hardly credible, however, that they used such language as that in the latter quotation unaided; yet it may well have been rendered in such terms by a scribe or lawyer recording the event.)

The question of personal bondage and the possibility of its removal was, naturally enough, raised more sharply and more directly in the uprisings of the later Middle Ages, such as in the violent Jacquerie of French peasants of 1358, which was precipitated by the military defeat of the nobility at Poitiers a couple of years before; and, even more specifically, in the English Peasant Revolt of 1381 and the German Peasant War of 1525. This advance in peasant ideology to the maturer form of voicing a demand for equality of status and freedom from villeinage as a right is noted by G. M. Trevelyan in his comment on the revolt of 1381: 'The rising of 1381 [he writes] sets it beyond doubt that the peasant had grasped the conception of complete personal liberty, that he held it degrading to perform forced labour, and that he considered freedom to be his right.'[5]

However, in all these late-medieval movements (as also in the Hungarian rising of 1514 led by Dózsa), the peasants found leaders from outside their ranks, and it appears that, in each case, the peasants' inherent ideology, arising directly from his deprivations and frustrations under seigneurial domination, was further enriched by the ideas of leaders who were generally sprung from the lower clergy or lesser nobility but often, too, from demobilized soldiers or from wealthier peasants who had won their freedom through commutation or had fallen out with the authorities.

The background to the events of 1381 in England is provided by the scarcity of labour occasioned by the Black Death of 1340 and the Hundred Years' War with the French which had already lasted, with intermissions, for forty years. The scarcity of labour had the effect of slowing down or reversing the process of commuting labour services for money rents which the lords had found advantageous when labour was abundant and the acquisition of ready money was a matter of first importance but, as the price of labour in the market rose, no longer found attractive. This reversal of liberalizing policies (expressed most notably in the restrictive Statutes of Labourers that were enacted by Parliament from 1346 on) was further aggravated by the levy (in 1380) of a poll tax of a shilling per head on all persons whether noble, bond or free. The levy, which naturally weighed most heavily on the poorer peasants (there had by now emerged a wealthier class of peasants employing labour of their own) was the spark which ignited the flame of revolt. The rising started with violent resistance to the collection of the tax in Essex, where the villagers first rioted and then murdered court officials sent to repress them. In June, riots spread throughout the county and, in Kent, armed rebels plundered the castle at Rochester and occupied Canterbury and opened its prison gates. The Kentishmen were led by Wat Tyler, an urban craftsman, and John Ball, a priest and principal ideologue of the movement, who set the tone of the rebellion by asking the challenging question, 'When Adam delved and Eve span, who was then the Gentleman?'

The men of Kent and Essex marched on London in separate columns, releasing more prisoners (including Ball himself) from the Marshalsea and King's Bench prisons at Blackheath.

'There followed,' the *Cambridge Medieval History* records, 'definite treachery in the city Government itself'; and, with such assistance, the rebels entered the city at two places, opened more prisons and sacked and destroyed properties belonging to the principal targets of their hatred, John of Gaunt, Hales the Treasurer, and lawyers fairly generally. Hales suffered the greater penalty; he and the Chancellor, Sudbury, were soon after dragged through the streets and beheaded on Tower Hill.[6]

Meanwhile, the royal council had decided on a more conciliatory course, and a meeting was arranged between the boy-King Richard II and Wat Tyler and his rebels at Mile End. Here it was agreed that villeinage and feudal services should be abolished while land held by villein tenure should be rented as freehold; also that monopolies and restrictions on buying land should be ended. The next day sterner councils prevailed; and, at a second meeting, Walworth, the mayor of London, mortally wounded Tyler, which was followed by the extraordinary episode of the young King riding into the rebels' ranks and promising to take Tyler's place and be their leader. It was a well-chosen gesture as the rebels (as so often in peasant risings) had no grievance against the King and welcomed his offer. So they were caught in a trap, retreated north to Clerkenwell and peacefully dispersed.

But news travelled relatively slowly, and it took some time before the bad news of Tyler's murder reached the counties north of London. So there was time for the 'good news' to reach them first that the King had freed all serfs and abolished feudal services; and as this news, borne by riders speeding through the country lanes, reached the villages it aroused the peasants in other districts to follow the Kentishmen's and Essex men's example. Risings took place in East Anglia on 12 June (on the very day of the first Mile End meeting) and, five days later, in Cambridgeshire and Hertfordshire. In Cambridgeshire, the peasants' principal grievance was the exaction of excessive manorial dues and, in twenty villages, bonfires were lit to burn documents belonging to unpopular landowners; and, in interesting anticipation of the more famous events that were to occur in France in the summer of 1789, in some villages the burning of documents was accompanied by the pillage and destruction of the manor house itself. Again, as in London, attacks were made on officials associated with the collection of the hated poll tax, as well as on justices and lawyers; but, once more as in the Great Fear of 1789, in Cambridgeshire, where, as Oman records, 'every form of violence abounded', the peasants were remarkably restrained in the justice they dispensed on persons, and only two deaths (one of Edmund Waller, a wealthy justice) are known for certain to have occurred.[7] The rebellion spread northward into the towns and villages of Yorkshire; but the loss of the principal leaders (for Ball, among others, had been imprisoned again) had given fresh heart to the Government and the nobility; and it was all over by the end of June, the rebellion having lasted a bare month.

We have noted certain similarities between the English Peasant Revolt and other rebellions of the time or of centuries later: the veneration of the person of the King and hatred for his 'evil' counsellors; careful discrimination in the selection of victims (here utterly at variance with the more bloody antics of the less organized Jacquerie); the destruction of documents recording the peasants' obligation to their lords, both in the village square and together with the manor house itself. But other features were peculiar to the event and to the circumstances out of which the Rebellion arose. One was the exaction of the poll tax, that, contrary to some peasant uprisings of the time, united the villagers and townsmen in a common cause. This is clearly evident from the composition of the rebels and from the active connivance of highly-placed London citizens in their entry into the city on 11 June. The relations of Londoners with Essex – where the main grievance was serfdom – were particularly close: it appears from a report prepared by the Middlesex Sheriffs that two London butchers (among others) had, since 30 May, been travelling around the county giving the call to arms: 'To London!' 'If these Londoners,' writes one historian of the event, 'did not create the revolt in Essex, they at least organized and directed it and gave it the precise objective which their hatred had chosen.'[8] Nor, as has already become amply evident, can the peasants themselves, who formed the shock-troops of the rebellion, be classified as forming a single group or class. Among the participants, there were the serfs whose main grievance, as in Essex, was villeinage itself. Elsewhere, the main support was given by former villeins who had won their freedom through a commutation of their services but found their wages restricted by the Statutes of Labourers; and, again, there were wealthier peasants whose main complaint was that the Statutes of Labourers not only kept wages low but favoured the lords by restricting the mobility of the labour they wished to hire. But the central issue, overshadowing all others, was that of serfdom itself; for it was the determination of the lords – and of the Government that protected their interests – to bind the serfs more closely to them after the Black Death that lay at the heart of the whole Rebellion. And to return briefly to the peasants' ideology: it appears (as Trevelyan noted) that it was their own experience of the dashing of their hopes through the nobiliar reaction since the 1350s which, laced with the preaching of John Ball, the 'crazy' Kentish priest, made them receptive to the notion that personal liberty and equality of status were no longer an elusive mirage but (given the right circumstances) an attainable goal.

The German peasants in 1525 had far more opportunities than the English peasants of 1381 to leave a number of faithful records of what their rebellion sought to achieve. The most important of these was the Twelve Articles of Swabia, composed on the south-western peasants' behalf in the town of Memmingen by a journeyman furrier between 27 February and 1 March 1525. And even more than the English Rebellion, the German Peasant War emerged out of a deep religious controversy – the Reformation – precipitated by Luther's famous Theses of half-a-dozen years before; so that, inevitably, the movement reflected the demand for a greater freedom within the Church which, in most of the peasant manifestoes, appeared side by side with the demand for the abolition of serfdom and the more onerous of feudal services and dues; and, inevitably, too, an important part in the direction and organization of the peasants' armies was played by pastors who owed their inspiration to Luther or his more militant lieutenants. In fact, the nucleus of peasant organization was formed by the Christian Unions, which, on a strictly provincial basis, welded together the numerous brotherhoods or alliances of protestant believers that had sprung up in the wake of the Lutheran Reformation. These Unions had the four-fold objective of recruiting new members, presenting a common front against the nobility, conducting military operations, and putting into effect the desired reforms. In all, the Unions were able to muster, within a month of the outbreak, no less than 300,000 armed adherents in the south-western region of Germany alone. In addition, there were smaller groups of rebels, emerging spontaneously without the guidance of the Lutheran pastors, who attracted or impressed their own local leaders – craftsmen, tradesmen, lesser clergy and the like – to give them cohesion, draw up demands and help them to define more sharply their ideology of protest.[9]

The German Peasant War, however, had origins going back far earlier than the Lutheran challenge. It was the last of a long series of peasant 'conspiracies', having a common origin in the increased feudal exploitation which, as in England, was a feature of the time. In the estates of Swabia, in the south-western Black Forest, and in Upper Alsace, both regions that became centres of peasant revolt, serfdom had become more strictly enforced or (as also in England a century before) reintroduced where it had been in decline, the right to tenancies had been curtailed, feudal dues increased in response to the rise in city prices, and access to the commons restricted. Besides, it is significant that these areas of revolt lay near to towns and were areas where relations between town and country were unusually close, and the south-west in particular had seen a rapid growth in population; and this, in turn, had sharpened social differentiation in the villages, raising the status of the wealthier peasant and driving the middle and smallholding peasant towards pauperization.

In 1476, the first in this series of peasant 'conspiracies' occurred in the Bishopric of Würzburg, a centre notorious for bad and oppressive government, where, under the influence of a young shepherd-musician turned preacher, known as 'Hans the Piper', the movement at first took a religious-ascetic turn and, inspired by Hans's preaching, attracted gatherings of 40,000 and more peasants at the shrine of the Virgin at Niklashausen. But Hans, who had other aims in mind, soon went into partnership with two Knights, Kunz of Thurnfeld and his son Michael, and with their aid turned the devout peasant pilgrims into a body of armed insurgents, whose aim it should be to capture the Bishop of Würzburg's castle. Of 34,000 armed men that responded to the Piper's call, over a half laid down their arms and dispersed peacefully when the Bishop, appearing with an armed force, promised reforms; and the rest were sent home soon after, leaving Hans as a prisoner who was later to be burned at the stake.

The next important rising was a highly organized affair in 1502, known as the *Bundschuh* (or Union Shoe), which followed other more limited outbreaks of the past seventy years that bore the same name. The earlier *Bundschuh* revolts had been largely concerned with resistance to taxes; but that of 1502 found a model organizer in a young serf (this was an unusual phenomenon at this time), Joss (Joseph) Fritz, from Untergrombach near Bruhsal. Joss successfully combined the strong religious feelings of his fellow peasants with the realization of the need to make a frontal assault on feudalism itself. His programme was, in the name of 'divine justice', to abolish all oppression and lordship, to end serfdom, dissolve abbeys and monasteries, and to end for ever the payment of rents, tithes, tolls or taxes; and waters, meadows and woods were to be made common to all. Its central theme was: 'Nothing but the justice of God', which meant, of course, that the existing feudal order must be destroyed. But the movement was betrayed and the *Bundschuh* subdued; and both Emperor and princes were thoroughly alarmed and called for exemplary punishment to be meted out to both participants and accomplices. However, Joss Fritz managed to elude his pursuers and organized a new *Bundschuh* in Breisgau, along the Rhine, in 1513. This time, he extended his programme to appeal to wider circles in both town and country. However, the plan was again betrayed; and, once more, Joss survived to form a third conspiracy – a further *Bundschuh* – in 1517, only to be betrayed again. In Württemburg, a similar movement, known as that of *Armer Konrad* (Poor Conrad, a peasant nickname) and this time involving townsmen as well as villagers, met a like fate in 1514.

The Peasant War of the next decade was able to learn lessons from both types of movement. On the one hand, the secret society, with its constant risk of being betrayed from within, was abandoned for the mass movement of peasants with elected – or appointed – leaders; and, on the other, the limited regional movement was succeeded by one with a far wider radius of operations. And, of course, in addition, there had by 1525 appeared the phenomenon of Martin Luther who, much to his alarm and disgust, was adopted as their inspiration and leader-in-chief by the rebellious peasants.

The rising began in early February 1525 in the Black Forest near Freiburg. By early March it had spread over most of Swabia, Franconia and Thuringia and went on to reach south into the Tyrol and east into Carinthia. Meanwhile, an army of 300–400,000 insurgents, based on six armed camps, were operating in Upper Swabia alone; cities were also involved and it was in the town of Memmingen, in Allgäu that (as we have said) the Twelve Articles were proclaimed in the name of all the south-western Swabian peasants centred in Upper Allgäu. Later rebellions followed and, by mid-April, the War engulfed an area equivalent to two-thirds of the whole of Germany.

The Twelve Articles of Swabia, which, more than any other, became the official manifesto of rebellion, was not a particularly militant document. It began (as others did, too) with an assertion of the right to freedom within the Church – in this case taking the form of a demand that pastors should be freely elected by their flocks. There followed a number of demands to curb the operation of feudalism: such as to restrict the payment of tithe, to abolish serfdom, to restore the peasant's traditional right to hunt and to cut wood from the forest, to abolish heriot and restrict labour service, to pay fair rents, to restore the fair dispensation of justice by the courts, and to respect the traditional common rights in field and forest. So, while the peasants demanded their personal freedom, they showed hostility to feudalism's excesses rather than to the feudal system itself.[10]

Other manifestoes that followed were often more militant in tone; and this, Engels suggests, depended on the presence in the camps of a core of revolutionary peasants subscribing to the more radical programme of Thomas Münzer, Luther's former associate but now bitter opponent.[11] But these were in a small minority and the bulk of the peasants, having voiced their demands, drifted home leaving their spokesmen to negotiate with the magistrates and princes. Engels, while recognizing that this was a major weakness on the peasants' part, also believed that another debilitating element was formed by the considerable number of footloose townsmen and unemployed villagers ('vagabond masses of the low-grade proletariat') who drifted into their camps and showed more willingness to talk than fight. This, he insists, severely demoralized the peasants.[12]

Meanwhile, the princes, after a slow start, had – with Luther's blessing – mobilized their armies and gradually mopped up the rebels that were still in the field, region by region, without encountering any large-scale or determined opposition. Thomas Münzer, still only twenty-eight years old, was captured in Thuringia in May and broken on the rack by his princely captors. The last engagements took place in Swabia and Franconia in late July; and, with these, the last of the peasant bands surrendered and the Peasant War, after six months of rebellion, was brought to an end.

Finally, how do we assess the ideology of the very heterogeneous armies of this Peasant War? It was, not surprisingly, as disparate as the composition of the armies themselves. On the one hand, there were the bulk of the peasants, smallholders for the most part, who were not prepared to fight outside their own districts but were certainly eager, whether by struggle or by negotiation, to win personal freedom from serfdom, to restrain the lords from solving their own financial problems at the peasants' expense by increasing burdensome taxes and services, and to ensure that old traditions were respected and that justice should be fairly administered. (So there was something here of both a backward and a forward-looking attitude.) There were others, of course, like Engels's 'vagabond masses', who were more concerned with wages than with services or taxes and more perhaps with the loot to be garnered from the beleaguered monasteries and castles than with liberation for themselves or for anyone else. In addition, there was the small militant minority, followers of Thomas Münzer, who aimed to create a cooperative commonwealth or to hold goods in common and whose sights, therefore, were raised much higher than the mere overthrow of feudalism. And, on the fringes of the Peasant War, were the knights and lesser nobility, who had already fought a war of their own ('the Knights' War') against the feudal nobility and often sided with the peasants; and also the burghers of the cities, several of them in open rebellion, whose anti-feudalism was probably limited to the quest for free markets and elective institutions.

So the German Peasant War, in terms of history, fulfilled two roles. As is evident enough, it played a not insignificant part in the history of German peasant movements and the development of a peasant ideology with personal freedom at its core. In addition, it may be seen – as Engels and some modern German historians of the event have seen it – as a part of the economic, religious and social crisis of the Reformation, that marked an important stage in the long period of transition from feudalism to capitalism.[13] But it was a comparatively early stage, as capitalism – at that time the only possible successor to feudalism – only became firmly established in Germany over two centuries later. And, for the present, the bourgeoisie, even those most solidly entrenched within their Free Cities, won nothing from the War; the old feudal nobility and clergy lost much of their property; and the peasants, for all their struggles, gained nothing as the concessions promised in the heat of battle were withdrawn once the crisis was past; and they were plunged back into the system of bondage from which they had attempted to escape. It was only the princes (so Engels concludes his account) that were the real victors, having successfully – with Luther's help – settled accounts with the old unreformed clergy, the feudal magnates, and the rebellious peasants who, to attain their freedom, had to wait another two centuries and more.[14]

NOTES

1. Rodney H. Hilton, 'Peasant Society, Peasant movements and Feudalism in Medieval Europe', in Henry A. Landsberger (ed.), *Rural Revolt: Peasant Movements and Social Change*, London, 1974, p. 69.
2. Hilton, p. 76.
3. ibid., p. 75.
4. ibid., p. 78.
5. G. M. Trevelyan, *England in the Age of Wycliffe*, p. 185; cit. Betty and Henry Landsberger, 'The English Peasant Revolt of 1381', in H. Landsberger (ed.), *Rural Revolt*, pp. 127–8.
6. This account and what follows is largely taken from the *Cambridge Medieval History*, vol. 7; cit. B. and H. Landsberger, in H. Landsberger (ed.), pp. 96–8.

7. Sir Charles Oman, *The Great Revolt*; cit. B. and H. Landsberger, p. 98.

8. C. Petit-Dutaillis, Introduction to *Le soulèvement des travailleurs d'Angleterre en 1381*, Paris, 1898, p. lxxii; cit. B. and H. Landsberger, p. 123.

9. Henry Cohn, 'The Peasantry of Swabia, 1525', in Janos Bak (ed.) *The German Peasant War*, Special Issue of *Journal of Peasant Studies*, 3 (October 1975), 12–13.

10. Cohn, in *JPS*, 3, 14–18.

11. F. Engels, *The Peasant War in Germany*, in *The German Revolutions*, Chicago, 1967, pp. 77–9.

12. Engels, p. 80. The point is disputed by other historians, who, broadening the area of discussion, point to the example of modern China, where Mao's armies were largely recruited among the 'uprooted'. (See, e.g. Edward Friedman, in *JPS* Special Issue on the Peasant War, vol. 3, pp. 121–2.) There is, however, plenty of evidence from other revolutions that supports Engels's view.

13. See a number of contributors to the Peasant War issue of *JPS*, vol. 3, esp. R. Wohlfeil, E. Engelberg, and G. Vogler, pp. 98–116.

14. Engels, pp. 114–17.

2

Under Absolute Monarchy

By the time of what is commonly called the Ancien Régime in Europe, when absolute monarchy, in one or other of its various forms, was most commonly in the saddle, the feudalism discussed in the previous chapter had undergone a number of changes. In Western Europe, it was on the wane in the sense that military tenures were a thing of the past and that serfdom had disappeared completely in England and was a rapidly diminishing factor in France, West Germany and Spain. In Eastern Europe, however, serfdom, far from being on the wane, was in its ascendancy, particularly in Russia, where serfdom (or, more properly, 'chatteldom') rapidly spread in Catherine II's day as the Empire expanded south and west and made fresh conquests at the expense of the Poles and Turks. But in all countries where serfdom survived and where the old feudal system of land tenure persisted, even in a modified form, the peasant continued to suffer the indignity of paying a multiplicity of services and dues – and even more than ever during the second 'feudal reaction' of the late eighteenth century – and where he suffered the further humiliation of being treated and despised as an inferior being. It was in the eighteenth century – under absolute monarchy or princely rule – that the peasants of Hildesheim, in Germany (so Jerome Blum tells us), performed no fewer than 138 separate obligations to their lord, whilst it has been claimed that in Livonia 356 work-days were devoted to their masters by each peasant household; and even in relatively emancipated France, where the peasants generally fared better than elsewhere, Turgot, when intendant at Limoges, reckoned that its landholding peasants paid 50 to 60 per cent of their gross annual income in taxes to the King and in dues to their *seigneurs*.[1]

So it is hardly surprising that, under absolute monarchy as under medieval Kings, unemancipated peasants continued to challenge the greed or brutality of their lords and, on frequent occasions, to demand their freedom from all personal restraints. But the more common feature of peasant revolt in the 'age of absolutism' was the challenge to state or monarch over the payment of taxes rather than to the seigneur over dues and obligations, or even over personal servitude. The reason, of course, is not so hard to find: the obligations to the lord were a perennial grievance which would eventually be settled by peasant rebellion; whereas the age in which Louis XIV built Versailles and other rulers built Sans Souci, Schönbrunn and St Petersburg, was also one of costly wars between the larger states in Europe when vast sums were expended on keeping the armies in the field and in expanding the state machine to the greater glory of the absolute ruler or 'enlightened despot'; France, Prussia, Austria and Russia in this respect all had a common experience; and in most (Prussia was the great exception) there were large-scale peasant revolts, often supported and sometimes led by other discontented elements within the clergy or aristocracy.

To illustrate the point let us take examples from Russia, Austria and France and attempt to see not only what the peasants did but (as far as our somewhat disparate sources will permit) what was in their heads. In Russia, where the modern nation-state had only begun to emerge, after a long period of misrule and disputed successions, under the Romanovs in the early seventeenth century, these internal struggles were far more bitter and violent than elsewhere. The revolt led by Stepan (Stenka) Razin, the first of the two great rebellions of the time, sprang directly from the efforts of the first two Romanov Tsars, Mikhail (1613–45) and his son Aleksei (1645–76), to build up a unitary state based on Moscow under conditions of continuous wars with their neighbours. The attempt involved the raising of burdensome taxes, the restriction of traditional liberties (including the peasants' right to enjoy a considerable degree of personal freedom), the curtailment of the marauding activities of the Cossack bands; not to mention the reorganization of the Orthodox Church at the expense of the Roskols (or Old Believers) and the elevation to high office of 'new' men recruited outside the ranks of the old noble ('boyar') class, leading to scandalous depredations at the public expense which outraged conservative opinion and inflicted increasing misery on the hard-pressed peasants. So, naturally enough, these injured and outraged elements sooner or later played some part in Stenka

Razin's revolt, which broke out in the Volga Valley some time in 1667. Stenka belonged to the upper class of the Old Cossacks based on the Don, and it was from their ranks that his earliest recruits were drawn. But his was a snowball movement which went on to swell its numbers from escaped serfs, Roskols subject to government persecution, urban craftsmen, petty merchants and footloose soldiers; and it was a motley army thus composed that appeared, a few months later, before the southern fortress-city of Astrakhan, which he eventually conquered and turned into a Cossack republic. By now (about 1669), he had begun to appear as a defender of the oppressed and, in September 1670, as he moved north to capture Nizhny-Novgorod, Tambov and Penza, he used these towns to launch a great peasant revolt in the whole area enclosed by the loop in the middle Volga. In the villages the peasants rose, put down their lords, plundered the land, destroyed their property, and formed themselves into marching bands that often joined up with Stenka's army as it moved north and west towards Moscow.

Meanwhile, Samara and Saratov also fell; but Simbirsk refused to open its gates and Stenka was defeated by Prince Baryatinsky with an army of 70,000 tsarist troops in two bloody battles in October 1670, and forced to retreat to his original base in the Don marshes. The rebellion continued in a desultory fashion in half a dozen districts until the beginning of 1671; but as Razin's star waned and his totemic value dwindled, the Cossacks or Cherkassk turned against him, seized him in his island redoubt and, in April, sent him as a prisoner to Moscow, where he was hanged in June 1671.

What were the objects of Stenka Razin's rebellion and of the peasant rebels in particular? Razin himself appears to have extended his aims and to have radicalized his demands as the rebellion progressed and as new groups of supporters came onto the scene. His eventual programme included the destruction of the great hereditary nobility, the governors, and the bureaucracy and Muscovite machinery of state that operated all over Russia; but for the Tsar himself, in spite of his occasional republican pretensions, he always expressed undying loyalty and respect. He also appears to have envisaged, under a patriarchal Tsar, a sort of democracy of small proprietors; and this, of course, is where the peasants, having been released from serfdom and relieved of their feudal burdens, would come in. So Razin's aims were revolutionary but certainly utopian, as he had no alternative machinery of state, and had no plan to create one, to put in the place of the old.

And what of the peasants' role in the affair? Were they called upon to play any active part in their own liberation? Very little, apart from killing off their lords, as we have seen; and there is no evidence (from Roland Mousnier's account, at least) that the peasants had any clear ideology beyond their hatred of the system that oppressed them and the more positive aspiration to see it ended – magically, as it were, by accepting Stenka's proffered hand to give them liberation.[2]

The rebellion of Emelyan Pugachev, an illiterate Cossack soldier, which broke out in September 1773 and ended in December 1774, falls within the same tradition. It also began among the Cossacks whose liberties had been still further curtailed; it had the same snowball quality and made the same widespread millenarial appeal, promising redress for the Old Believers and freedom for the Bashkir nation lying to the east of the Urals, and it provoked a peasant revolt (including this time the peasant-workers in the Ural foundries); and Pugachev, like Razin, having captured a number of fortresses and having marched north and west to the Volga, led a mixed force of Cossacks, peasants, Old Believers, bandits and footloose wanderers in the direction of Moscow, the traditional capital (though by now superseded as capital, since Peter's time, by St Petersburg). Both movements provoked a smilar panic among the rulers and compelled them – belatedly – to marshal their forces and send an army to head the rebels off from the capital, and beat them in the field. In both cases, too, the leader, having been worshipped almost as a god, was captured by his own followers, securely bound and handed to the authorities for execution once his mortality had become evident and his value as a totem had been destroyed.

But there were two important differences. Where Stenka Razin had called himself a republican to win Cossack support and had been satisfied with the title of 'gosudar', which could equally be applied to a high official like the Patriarch Nikon, Pugachev claimed – as so many 'False Dmitris' in the Time of Troubles had done before him – to be the 'true Tsar' – in this case, Peter III who had been murdered by the Palace Guard with the connivance of Catherine, his wife and successor. Posing as the 'protector of the people' (responding to Peter's reputation among the peasants as the 'liberating Tsar'),* who had miraculously escaped his assassins' bullets, Pugachev won over the Cossacks in the district of Yaik in the southern Urals, and promised to restore their traditional liberties over which they were already in open revolt. He marched east, where he made similar promises of freedom to the Bashkir people and to the Old Believers, and moved up the Volga to bring a similar message to that given by Razin in 1670 to the serfs (accounting for half the population) and the state peasants along the middle reaches of the Volga. But – and this was the second difference – he also liberated the most class-conscious of the peasant groups – the peasant-workers in the Ural factories and mines.[3]

Like Razin's, Pugachev's movement lacked a coherent revolutionary programme, being made up of a medley of often disparate elements, but it put forward a number of reasonably well-defined goals corresponding to the interests of the multiplicity of groups that flocked to his banner. They included (as voiced by the leader at various stages of his rebellion) sending Catherine into a nunnery, the removal of oppressive taxes and other burdens from the people's backs, the expropriation of the *pomeshchiki* (the landowning gentry and the peasants' *bête noire*), to punish the boyars and officials for their 'hospitality' (an ironic twist), to restore old customs including the faith of the Old Believers, and to extend Cossack liberties to the common people at large. The last point was the most positive of the demands and one very similar to one of Razin's: to replace the corrupt government and institutions of Catherine II by a Cossack-style democracy which, presumably, would entail the abolition of serfdom and forced labour in industry.

We may assume that this latter point corresponded closely to the peasants' own wishes: their frequent wild outbursts of hatred against the hated *pomeshchiki* most certainly suggest it. More certainly, the indentured peasant labourers working in the Urals foundries and mines believed that freedom could be won

---

* During a short reign Peter's decrees of February 1762 had converted monastery serfs into state peasants, taken over Church lands, temporarily suspended the campaign against Old Believers and reduced the price of salt.

by struggle; in the decades preceding the rebellion there had been numerous strikes protesting against the near-slave conditions imposed by N. Demidov and other rapacious employers; and it sounds credible enough that when Pugachev's lieutenants read out his 'freedom' manifesto in the south Urals factory zone, workers that heard it (so reads an official report) 'cried out, "Glad to serve him, the Tsar" and 500 men gathered, volunteers to serve Pugachev'.[4] Elsewhere, in the villages to the west of the Volga (it was further reported) peasants gathered and cried that 'the time was coming when they would take the upper hand over the authorities and there would be nothing to fear whatever they did'. And, more specifically, it was also reported from the Volga that the peasants believed 'if it were possible to hand all the *pomeshchiki*, then there would be freedom for all . . . and there would be no soul and other taxes, recruiting levies [or] state sales [monopolies]'.[5]

Such reports, presented by Philip Longworth, suggest that the Russian peasants of 1774 shared the punitive violence of the spontaneous *jacquerie* with their forebears of a century before; but also that, given the dramatic intrusion into the village of Pugachev's men, their goals had become extended and more precisely defined. Yet it was only the factory peasants that had begun to take the initiative under their own leaders (however transitory) and to give evidence of an ideology that came close to resembling the relative sophistication of the English peasants of 1381.

Outside Russia, the most sustained of the peasant rebellions in southern and eastern Europe at this time were those in the Austrian dominions. Unlike the Russian example, they were initiated by the peasants themselves and they broke out in response to the promise of agrarian reform from above rather than to the promises of an outside leader at a time of intense oppression and political crisis. Broadly, they fall into two main groups: those preceding (or anticipating) Joseph II's historic agrarian reforms and those following in their wake. Among the first was a peasant rebellion in Silesia directed against the *Robot*, or compulsory labour services, in the Empress Maria Theresa's time, in 1767. Four years later, the first of the *Robot* Patents (decrees) was applied to Silesia. But it was not yet proclaimed elsewhere though rumours were already rife that Joseph, who had been co-ruler with his mother since 1765, was planning a general charter of peasant 'liberties'. Fed by this rumour, an uprising took place in Bohemia in 1775 when 15,000 peasants marched on Prague; and it was surely more than a coincidence (and indicative of peasant regard for Joseph) that they chose as their leader a young man who bore a striking resemblance to the Emperor himself. They demanded that the officials and landlords should immediately put into effect the charter which they mistakenly believed had already been proclaimed at Vienna. So the demonstration was one of support for, rather than in opposition to, the Imperial Government, and to reward the peasants for their confidence the standard *corvée* was now applied to Bohemia as it had been applied to Silesia before, while Maria Theresa ordered that the old manual *Robot* be commuted to a monetary payment on her private estates.

Maria Theresa was only a limited reformer, but once his mother had died (in 1780), Joseph, who had the peculiarity among all despots – whether 'benevolent' or other – of having a genuine desire to improve the peasant's lot, began to put his plans into operation. They took the form of three Patents. The first, the Strafpatent, limited the lord's right to punish his peasant; the second and the most important, the Emancipation Patent, abolished personal servitude by giving the peasant the right to leave the estate and marry whom he pleased (it did not altogether abolish labour service though it restricted its extension); and the third, the Taxation Patent, ordered the substitution of a monetary payment for the *corvée* in kind – but it applied only to peasants on 'rustical' (or non-demesne) lands and to those paying a land tax of at least two florins a year, thus excluding something like one half of the peasant population.

So the Patents, as they were applied in stages between 1781 and 1789, proved a disappointment; moreover, there was the usual bureaucratic delay in carrying out the laws, so that neither landlords nor officials, uncertain where they stood in the matter, were enthusiastic about the provisions. In consequence, rebellions followed both of peasants excluded by the law and of those impatient to enjoy it. In 1784 there was a revolt of excluded peasants in Transylvania (though this, in addition, had religious and ethnic undertones) and in 1786 in Moravia; and, in 1789, of Austrian peasants grown impatient with the long delays. A more despairing outcry was provoked by Joseph's decision, after facing rebellion from his noble subjects in Hungary and elsewhere, to withdraw the provisions of his Emancipation decree of 1789 a year after it had been passed; all the more despairing as many tenants, in anticipation of enjoying its benefits, had sold their team of oxen and naturally thought they had been let down badly. There followed a widespread refusal to render *Robot* at all; but the peasants' spirits, elated by the hope of a better life to come, had been crushed and no overt rebellion followed.[6] So emancipation became an item of unfinished business that would not be realized until the revolution of 1848.

In France, under the absolute monarchy of the three Louis, peasant revolt had a more varied history than in Austria and Russia; but there, as in Russia, resentment against high taxes played a major part. Above all, in France, to lend greater variation to rebellion, a far greater social differentiation had developed within the peasantry than in Russia or the Austrian dominions. At the top there had already emerged a *kulak*-style peasantry distinguished from their fellows by their greater wealth and ability to sell at higher prices in the market. In the middle there were the mass of small proprietors (the *laboureurs*) many of whom did not hold enough land to produce for the market at all. Lower down were the *métayers* (sharecroppers) who were generally poor, often as poor as the landless peasants whose whole livelihood depending on working for others as *journaliers* and who held the lowest status in the village. The interests of these groups naturally varied: the wealthier peasants (the *coqs de village*) were hostile to those traditional collective rights (such as gleaning or *vaine pâture*) which stood in the way of their extending their holdings (yet they resisted the dividing up of the common lands, which served them well as easily accessible pasture); the 'middling' to poorer proprietors were the most stalwart of the upholders of collective rights; while the sharecroppers and the landless – or even the poorest of the peasant proprietors – being short of land, would have been happy to be allotted a portion of the commons and also, having no surplus to sell, were interested in low food prices and (if *journaliers*) that wages should not lag behind the price of bread. Yet there were two issues over which the village generally stood united: the first, high taxes that were a burden to all, and the second the persistence of the feudal land system with its proliferation of obligations and dues, which prevented even the wealthiest and most independent *coq de village* from feeling that his land was really his own. So, as we have seen already from the examples of Austria and Russia, either of these issues could rouse the peasants as a body and impel them to act together. In addition, when harvests were bad and prices rose, the poorest peasants tended to break ranks and to act on their own against the *accapareur* (or hoarder) who temporarily replaced the *seigneur* or *gabeleur* as the villager's worst friend.[7]

In the seventeenth century – when taxation to pay for Richelieu's and Louis XIV's wars was the dominant issue – the *gabeleur* or other type of *taxateur* became the main target of peasant violence. Roland Mousnier and other historians have paid attention to half-a-dozen major movements: the Bordeaux riots of 1635, the *Croquants* in Saintonge and Périgord in 1636–7, the *Va-Nu-Pieds* in Normandy in 1639; and then – after the lull provided by the two Frondes and the early years of Louis XIV's personal rule – the renewal of anti-salt tax rioting in Brittany and Bordeaux. Historians have not seen eye to eye on the significance of these movements and there have therefore been differences in their conclusions. Thus, the Soviet historian, Boris Porchnev, who has made the most thorough study of all the riots up to 1650, insists that, while the peasants were supported, and often led, by townsmen and country gentry, it should be treated as a specifically peasant movement, arising primarily out of the peasants' hostility (far more consistent than that of the dissident gentry) to exorbitant taxes and feudal exactions.[8] Roland Mousnier, on the other hand, best noted as a historian of administration, places far greater emphasis on the 'outside' influence, initiative and guidance of the towns and aristocracy, reducing the peasants' role to one of subservience and of waiting on events; yet he grudgingly concurs: 'Of course, I realize that the peasants were quite capable of rebelling on their own against the tax burdens. Nevertheless, the activity of the lords in this connection, and especially of the country squires, is irrefutable in many instances.'[9]

In most of these episodes, the tax that stirred particular fury was the *gabelle*, or tax on salt, which had the peculiarity that it had to be paid on a certain fixed quantity of salt whether one wanted to buy it or not, and which in some regions (*the pays de la grande gabelle*) was far more burdensome than it was in others. In the 1630s it was the Croquants – the 'poor countrymen' – that became most prominently engaged in protest, first at Bordeaux and Agen in 1635, later at Saintonge and in Poitou in 1636 and Périgord in 1637. What was in the rioters' minds is clear enough both from their violent action against the *gabeleurs* and the slogans reported by officials. At Angoulême the cry was 'Down with the Gabelle!'; and, at Agen the year before, 'Death to the *gabeleurs*!', 'Kill the *gabeleurs*!' and (significant of traditional loyalties) 'Vive le Roi et sans gabelles!' In addition, the *Croquants* of Saintonge affirmed (though this may not be the peasants speaking for themselves) that they were 'good Frenchmen' and would not receive into their company any lord or prince disaffected from the King's Court, and made clear from their statement of demands that they were not looking for reform but for a return to the good old customs existing before the days they began to be harassed by *gabeleurs* and other rapacious officials.[10] Porchnev adds another observation: that with the *Croquant* movement of the early seventeenth century peasant revolt had become secular and lost the religious trappings so familiar to the century before.[11]

The *Va-Nu-Pieds* movement (1639), which drew its name from the barefooted salt makers of Avranches and Coutances in west Normandy, was also directed against the *gabelle* and derived its main rank-and-file support from peasants and saltmakers, and found its leaders among the poor gentry and parish priests. One of these, Jean Morel, parish priest of Saint-Gervais in Avranches, served as the movement's principal publicist and as secretary to the apocryphal Jean-Nu-Pieds himself – a name reminiscent of the Ludds, Swings and Rebecca's and other composite heroes in a long tradition of anonymous leaders of popular revolt.[12]

But there were more than taxes at issue in peasant uprisings of the last twenty-five years of the 'Great Monarch's' reign, with its wars, famines and religious persecution. This was the age of the great peasant insurrection in Calvinist Languedoc, known as the war of the Camisards, the last of the French religious wars.[13] But it was more than that, because it was also fought over the peasant's manorial obligations to his lord; and, soon after, in

Catholic Quercy and Périgord, peasants were extending their field of operations in challenging the whole existing order by refusing to pay taxes to the King, tithe to the Church, or to perform servile manual labour for the upkeep of the roads. Louis' long reign ended in a final outburst of peasant riots over the disastrous harvest and famine of 1709 and further exactions of tax collectors for the War of Spanish Succession.

After 1709 (or, more exactly, around the mid-1720s), peasant rebellion, so familiar to observers in Louis XIII, Mazarin and Louis XV's time, became muted and did not reappear, and then with redoubled vigour, until the eve or outbreak of the French Revolution. Moreover, the chief object of peasant protest had changed and neither taxes nor feudal obligations played more than a secondary role in the *émotions* of the period 1730 to 1788. True enough, these grievances continued and did not lie entirely dormant, as shown by the study of the province of Savoy (admittedly, not a part of France until 1792) between 1650 and 1792 made by Jean Nicolas, a young French scholar. Nicolas shows that while open and violent protest against the seigneurial system fell off sharply after 1730, outbreaks against taxes, tithes, the royal *corvée* and encroachments of commons persisted, and it only needed the economic crisis, the seigneurial reaction and the political fermentation of the 1780s to bring all the old grievances to the surface, generalize protest, give it a sharper edge and put peasant rebellion once more on the order of the day.[14]

In the meantime, peasant protest took another form and the grain speculator (the *accapareur*) came into the picture; and it was no longer the prosperous or 'middling' peasant selling for the market but the poor peasant consumer, together with the wine-grower (who also had to buy his bread) and the small consumer in the city, that rioted when prices rose; and, at this stage, the food riot took over as the principal form of protest and remained so for the next sixty years. Among writers who have noted this phenomenon, Daniel Mornet, the 'cultural' historian, has recorded its appearance in forty individual years between 1724 and 1789 and, according to his calculations, it occurred in twenty-two of the twenty-six years between 1763 and 1789.[15] The most remarkable of these outbreaks was the so-called 'Flour War', which spread across half-a-dozen provinces around (and including) Paris in a little over two weeks in April and May 1775. The main demand – expressive of the small consumer's basic ideology – was for 'le pain à deux sols' (bread at two sous a pound) with proportionate reductions in the prevailing price of flour and grain; and it was widely believed – and this, above all, gave the riots their momentum – that the King himself had ordered that prices should come down; and with a certain modicum of justice, as the Prince de Poix, the Royal official at Versailles, had set the price of bread at the price demanded a few days after the riots began.[16] And this time, as in other riots of the kind, there was no outside assistance from other groups; the poor consumers, whether peasants or other, were left to fend for themselves.

How had this new situation come about? Briefly, as C.-E. Labrousse has amply attested, it happened for two reasons. First, because the rise in agricultural prices between the 1720s and 1770s had considerably benefited the large and 'middling' peasants, who had therefore been less inclined than in the century before to press their claims for less onerous taxes and feudal dues; and, second, because the poorer peasants, like all other small consumers, had no share in these benefits (in fact the reverse) and, as prices rose, they expressed their dissatisfaction through the traditional weapon of the food riot which, although it had been by no means abandoned in the stormier days of Richelieu and Louis, had been eclipsed by protest of a more violent form.[17]

So this was the situation for more than sixty years; but once market prices of grain and wine began to fall after the mid-1770s while industrial prices soared in the crisis of 1788, and the *seigneurs* sought compensation for both by turning the screw on their tenants in terms of increasing dues and obligations; and as the political crisis in the capital deepened, the village once more closed its ranks and, within the context of revolution, launched a massive nationwide rebellion against the whole manorial system. This time, the movement was all their own and it was their own spokesmen that presented the terrified *châtelains* with the order to destroy their records often purporting (as in 1775) to come from the King himself ('de par le Roy'). The newly created National Assembly, consisting of bourgeois and liberal-minded nobles, could not do other than bow before the storm;

but their own properties were often at stake, so they settled on a compromise which left a great deal of the old system untouched. As an English historian of the event has written:

> Could a medieval lawyer have been transported to the France of 1790 and told that Jacques Bonhomme, a peasant, was bound to carry his corn to the lord's mill [as he still was, if he had not bought his redemption], to perform so many *corvées* during the year, to pay *rachat* or *acapte* at each mutation of property, and that his land was subject to *champart* and *lods et ventes*, he would have unhesitantly proclaimed him a serf, and would have been filled with amazement to hear that he was nothing of the sort, but a free man.[18]

So there remained plenty more for the peasants to do; the task was only completed with the Jacobins' help in the summer of 1793. By this time, too, the peasants, like the townsmen before them, had long been exposed to the new revolutionary ideology. But this, like the Revolution itself, belongs to a later chapter.

NOTES

1. J. Blum, *The End of the Old Order in Rural Europe*, Princeton, 1978, pp. 50, 71.
2. Roland Mousnier, *Peasant Uprisings in Seventeenth-Century France, Russia and China* (English version of *Fureurs paysannes*), London, 1971, pp. 196–229.
3. For good accounts, see M. Raeff, 'Pugachev's Rebellion', in R. Forster and J. P. Greene (eds), *Pre-Conditions of Revolution in Early Modern Europe*, Baltimore, 1970; R. Portal, 'La Révolte de Pougachev', *Etudes d'hist. mod. et contemp.*, vol. 1, 1947; and P. Longworth, 'The Pugachev Revolt: The Last Great Cossack Peasant Rising', in H. Landsberger (ed.), *Rural Protest*, esp. pp. 195–220.
4. See Longworth, p. 196; and also R. Portal, *L'Oural au XVIIIe siècle*, Paris, 1950.
5. Longworth, pp. 197, 226.
6. E. M. Link, *The Emancipation of the Austrian Peasant 1740–1798*, London 1949; and E. Wangermann, *From Joseph II to the Jacobin Trials*, Oxford, 1959, *passim*.
7. Useful sources here are G. Lefebvre, *Etudes sur la révolution française*, Paris, 1954, pp. 246–68, and Barrington Moore, *Social Origins of Dictatorship and Democracy*, Boston, 1966, pp. 70–4.
8. B. Porchnev, *Les soulèvements populaires en France au XVIIe siècle*, Paris, 1972.
9. Mousnier, *Peasant Uprisings*, p. 52. For a discussion of this controversy, see

J. H. M. Salmon, 'Venal Office and Popular Sedition in Seventeenth-Century France', *Past and Present*, no. 37, 1967, pp. 21–43.

10. Mousnier, pp. 46, 57, 62.

11. Porchnev, p. 49. In England the case was quite different, as will be seen in a later chapter.

12. Mousnier, pp. 87–113.

13. For a brief but authoritative account, see Philippe Joutard, 'La Cévenne camisarde', *Histoire* (Paris), no. 1, May 1978, pp. 54–63.

14. J. Nicholas, 'Sur les émotions populaires au XVIIIe siècle: le cas de la Savoie', *Annales hist. de la Rév. française*, no. 214, 1973, pp. 593–607; no. 215, 1974, pp. 111–53.

15. D. Mornet, *Les origines intellectuelles de la Révolution française*, Paris, 1947, pp. 444–8.

16. For a short account, see G. Rudé, *The Crowd in History*, New York, 1964, pp. 22–32.

17. C.-E. Labrousse, Introduction to *La crise de l'économie française à la fin de l'ancien Régime et au début de la Révolution*, Paris, 1944, pp. ix–xli.

18. Sydney Herbert, *The Fall of Feudalism in France*, New York, 1969 (reprint), p. 130.

3

Latin America

One main difference between the peasant question in Latin America and that in the European countries we have been considering in the last two chapters is that, in Latin America from the sixteenth century on, the land was colonized by an alien power – in most cases, by Spain – which reduced the largely Indian native population to serve the foreign settlers as serfs or peons, working long hours for their foreign masters and enjoying little in the way of civil rights. A result has been that, in these countries, the peasant question has always carried racial overtones and that the struggle for economic freedom has always been accompanied or overlaid by a struggle for ethnic survival, one form of which has been – as among the Indian peasants in Colombia – a constant war on two fronts: on the one hand, against the large estates (or *haciendas*) and, on the other, against the encroachments of white or *mestizo* peasant settlers.[1] A second feature has been the deep chasm separating the relatively 'backward' and illiterate village from the modernizing and relatively forward-looking town or city; and a third that when unions appeared in the 1920s, as an emanation of the culture of the cities, they found a rural population to organize that was plunged in ignorance and superstition which it has taken the peasant movements half a century to overcome.[2]

The system of landholding in Latin America has, not surprisingly, borne the stamp of its colonial origins. The traditional pattern has been a tripartite one whose form naturally varies from one country to another (according to widely varying geographical and geological features), but which most commonly appears as follows: with the rich settlers (generally of Spanish origin) occupying *latifundia* or *haciendas* employing a large part of the rural population at the top; with the smallholders, or *rancheros*, holding small properties – often communely and with the constant danger of encroachment by the neighbouring *hacienda* – in the middle; while, at the bottom of the social pile were the great majority of peons, the landless labourers, holding tiny plots of kitchen-gardens but largely dependent for survival on the servile labour they perform so many days a week for the rich men on the large estates. In this system, an ever larger proportion of the acreage – whether of coffee or grain or pasture – tended to become the property of the *haciendas* whereas the small and 'middling' cultivators were left with an ever-decreasing share of the land. A survey of the conditions of land tenure in seven Latin American states recently conducted (in 1963) by the Interamerican Committee for Agricultural Development bears this out.[3] It shows that in Ecuador, Guatemala and Peru nearly nine in ten of the rural population are accounted for by *rancheros* and landless labourers and nearly two in three of the rest with the single exception of the more prosperous Argentina.[4] In theory at least, one saving grace for the poor and landless peasants has been traditionally provided by the communal lands and rights to which, as in medieval Europe, all members of the rural community has had access. But, in practice, owing to the rapacity of the *haciendados*, this has provided little security as an almost continuous feature of the Latin American rural scene has been the usurpation of these common lands – in what has been called the 'rape of the *pueblos*' – by the haciendas, either by means of direct seizure (as in Peru already in the eighteenth century) or, in more recent times, by the use of courts and legislatures that have generally proved to be compliant instruments in the owners' hands.

In consequence, failing effective legal redress, the peasants have most commonly – and here at variance with their European forebears – retaliated by reoccupying lands that were lawfully theirs; this has been perhaps the most common form of the class struggle in the Latin American village where militancy has, accordingly, been more often measured in terms of the number of land seizures by peasants rather than in terms of riot, or large-scale rebellion. Most of these outbreaks, before the appearance of peasant unions and cooperatives in the 1920s, were more or less spontaneous and local affairs, involving peaceable squatting in the first place but almost inevitably developing later, as the troops moved in, into violent confrontations at a great cost in peasant lives. Such movements took place in scattered areas of Mexico and Bolivia in the late nineteenth century; and, more recently, they have taken the form of the massive occupation of hacienda lands by thousands of insurgent peasants in the Peruvian highlands during the late 1940s and again in 1963–4;[5] and (even more sensationally) in the course of the bloody *Violencia* (or 'times of violence') in Colombia between 1949 and 1958, when whole communities, organized in this case not on a class but on a strictly 'client'-basis (according to their affiliation to the Conservative or Liberal parties) fought it out to a bloody conclusion, leaving a toll of between 100,000 and 200,000 lives.[5] Sometimes these encounters have proved utterly futile, as in the battles of the Colombian *Violenzia* which brought no advantage to the peasants – rather the reverse as it merely lined the pockets of the political manipulators in both of the warring factions and, by making it impossible for the unions to operate, left the peasants defenceless against further depredations. In the Central Sierras of Peru, however, particularly in La Convención Valley in the Department of Cuzco, peasants, led by their own village officials, won considerable successes by reclaiming – and retaining – 700,000 acres of pasture from the neighbouring haciendas between 1963 and 1965.[7]

More widespread movements of a national character have occurred, within the context of revolution, in Bolivia and Mexico. In Bolivia, before the great Reform of 1952, the hacienda-owners were a small white Spanish-speaking minority, allied with the local tin-barons, who exploited an Indian majority, most of whom were *colonos* (serfs) living on the hacienda who, in return for the right to farm small subsistence plots of their own, were obliged to work three or four days a week, usually with the help of their families, either on the hacienda itself or at the owner's town residence. In addition, a number of 'free' Indian communities had precarious control of common lands and, in return, did so many days of labour for the local authorities. It was these communities that bore the brunt of almost continuous usurpation; so it was on the loss of these rights that the earliest protest movements in Bolivia tended to be focused. One of these was led as early as 1898–9 by Zárate Willca, who was later assassinated by a Liberal Government that the peasants had helped to power. Another uprising, which took place in 1927, involved as many as 50,000 men but was crushed by the army after a month of struggle.

Unrest became more generalized – involving both Spanish and Indian-speaking peasants (though not often in unison) – after Bolivia's defeat by Paraguay in the Chaco War (1933–5). The whole Indian nation now began to mobilize under a succession of leaders, among them Jose Rojas, Luis Ramos Quevedo and Antonio Mamani Alvarez. They helped the peasants to raise their sights above the mere settlement of immediate grievances and to aspire to abolish peonage on the great estates and to a radical change in the whole (feudal) social and political structure. They organized unions and federations and – under Quevedo and Alvarez – summoned the first Indian Congress to meet at La Paz in May 1945. A civil war followed and, in August 1949, Alvarez circulated a leaflet calling on the Bolivian Indians, 'without distinction of social classes or sects of any kind', to engage 'in permanent revolution' until the Conservative Goverment had been overthrown and the country had been given a liberal constitution. Thus the peasant movement became an important auxiliary of the Liberal Government which, in 1953, adopted a constitution that began the long – and still not completed – process of ending peonage, breaking up the haciendas and redistributing the land among the former Indian serfs.[8]

In Mexico, peasant revolt and national revolution have been even more closely associated than in Bolivia. Before 1810 – the opening year of the Morelos-led revolution which gave the country its independence – the Mexican land system was similar to Bolivia's. Yet it had features of its own; of which the most important were that the *haciendados*, to add further to the peasants' fury, were often absentee owners and that the expanding hacienda, counting on the Government's protection, frequently invaded the freeholds of the *rancheros* and the Indians' communal holdings in order to swell their reserves of labour. It is therefore not surprising that when the liberal landowner, Francisco Madero, raised the banner of revolt and seized power from the Díaz dictatorship in 1910, the peasants leapt into action all over the country to win restitution of the lands that had been stolen from them. 'Madero,' observed the fallen dictator as he left for exile, 'has unleashed a tiger; let us see if he can control him'.[9]

In the event, the 'tiger' proved to be one of the most protracted and best organized peasant revolts of modern times –

and certainly the most sensational in Mexico's history – that led by Emiliano Zapata in the south and by Pancho Villa, one-time bandit, in the north. Zapata was the son of a small *ranchero*, born about 1875 in the village of Anenecuilco in the state of Morelos, lying south of Mexico City. His father farmed a small plot of communally held land, but he and his fellow-villagers lost their plots to the neighbouring hacienda. So, from an early age, Emeliano became involved in the villagers' attempts to retrieve them. At thirty, he was elected president of the village council; but because of the militancy of his actions – though at this stage entirely legal – he was sent to do military service in Mexico City, thus widening his horizons and providing him with a useful training for his future role as a peasant leader.

Returning to his village, Zapata formed a union between his own village and two others with similar problems. When legal action failed to gain redress, Zapata and his companions responded to Madero's call for revolution and helped to overthrow Díaz. However, it soon appeared that the new President's support for a solution of the agrarian problem in the interests of the small peasants was only lukewarm; so Zapata decided to strike out on his own and, in November 1911, he formulated an independent programme of land reform, known as the Plan of Ayala, and made war on Madero and his successors to achieve it. Meanwhile, his guerilla troops redistributed land according to his Plan in the areas that fell under their control; but they failed to follow up their successes by marching on the capital. So, inevitably, the tables were turned on Zapata when a new President of resolution – Carranza – took over the Government. In January 1915, Carranza 'stole' a large part of the Plan of Ayala, thus initiating the twenty-year history of Mexican land reform, and armed militant urban workers to quell the peasant revolt.[10] Zapata retired to the mountains south of the City, where he formed an alliance with Pancho Villa, the 'social bandit' turned guerrilla leader of a force of 20,000 men from the north, to continue the war against Carranza. *The New York Times*, sensitive to North-American interests, ominously declared in March 1919 that a return to normalcy in Morelos would depend upon 'the utter downfall, the permanent absence, or extinction of ZAPATA . . . he is beyond amnesty'.[11] Three weeks later, Zapata was tricked into an ambush and assassinated by a group of Carranza's officers; and the peasant rebellion began to peter out. A year after, Villa made his peace with Carranza's successor, Obregón, and retired to a farm where he was assassinated in turn in 1923.[12]

But reform 'from above' continued; and, in spite of the running battle fought by the hacienda-owners involving terror and assassination, the reform programme made headway under successive Presidents, peonage giving way to the mobility of free labour and the number of recipients of land – mainly peasants living in village communities – increasing from 7,733 per year in 1915–20 to 52,600 in 1921–34, and to 135,000 per year in 1935–40.[13] This final great burst (there were other minor ones to follow) came under the liberal-democratic régime of Lázaro Cárdenas, elected President in 1934. In Cárdenas the peasants at last found a genuine friend, who not only distributed land to the landless on a massive scale (in 1936 alone, 150,000 hectares – roughly twice as many acres – of irrigated land were distributed to 35,000 peasants in the cotton-producing region of Laguna), but he actually organized peasants in armed defence units to fight off the 'White Guards' set on foot by the landowners to arrest the onward march of reform. An Agrarian Code, serving as a comprehensive charter of peasants' rights, was adopted in 1934; and, four years later, the peasants, to show their gratitude, pledged their newly founded National Peasant Federation (C.N.C.) to give the Government their political support. It was the highest point reached in the Mexican Revolution, which, after Cárdenas ended his term in 1940, entered into a period of consolidation, which slowed the pace of reform and virtually brought the thirty-year long 'popular' phase of the Revolution to an end.[14]

As we have seen, this popular phase had quite distinctive qualities. On the one hand, in no other revolution (without even excepting the Chinese and the French) have the peasants played so important and so independent a role; and – this time excepting the French – in none other have peasants, through struggle and independent organization, achieved such an outstanding measure of success. Theirs was the programme of land reform, formulated in its essentials by Zapata at Ayala in 1911, 'stolen' by Carranza, to isolate Zapata and Villa, in 1915; and all but completed 'from above' – but with continuing peasant intervention – by Cárdenas after 1934. Yet, having said so much, we must admit that they had serious limitations when it came to taking power. The leaders of these peasant armies – Zapata, the peasant and son of a peasant, and Villa, the Robin Hood style bandit turned guerrilla leader – had no inclination to venture far from their native base – Morelos in the first case, Chihuahua in the second – nor to make any bid for power; and, only when forced by necessity, did they enter Mexico City from which they retreated at the earliest possible opportunity. As Eric Wolf explains it:

> Thus, while Villa's armies and Zapata's forces were instrumental in destroying the power of the Díaz régime and its epigonous successor Victoriano Huerta, they were themselves unable to take the decisive steps to institute a new order in Mexico. Zapata, because he was unable to trascend the demands of his revolutionary peasants, concentrated upon a narrow area of Mexico, and Villa gloried in warfare, but had no understanding for social and political exigencies. Symbolic of this tragic ineptitude of both parties is their historic meeting in Mexico City at the end of 1914 when they celebrated their fraternal union but could not create a political machine that could govern the country.[15]

In short, they had no desire to devise a constitution for Mexico to meet the needs of the small proprietors and working people as a whole. The peasants were their 'people' and land reform was the height of their ambition; and this, in the course of time, was what they won; and national politics and national political solutions they left to others, to middle-class liberals, lawyers, soldiers and the like. And that, for all their achievement (so history tells us) – and here the Mexican experience is no different from any other – is as far as peasant-led peasant movements could be expected to go.[16] (Mao's ability to lead a national peasant army to power – but with the constant aid of cadres from the cities – is something entirely different.)

And now what can be said of the ideology of the peasant movements of the past century in Latin America? Not surprisingly, there is no simple answer as the peasant experience has differed so widely between countries and generations. Yet, in the earlier movements we have mentioned, there was a certain uniformity; for, at this stage, whether we talk of Ecuador, Peru,

Bolivia or Mexico, the peasants' response to repression or to seizure of their lands was purely defensive and, as in 'pre-industrial' society elsewhere, they were committed to a restoration of the past: in this case to restore to their traditional owners the land, whether held singly or in common, that had been stolen or was being threatened with expropriation. Such an attitude – the desire to restore or maintain the past rather than to stake a claim for something new – persists until the present day. We may cite the example of the Indian shepherds in the Central Sierra of Peru, whom we find as recently as 1913 resisting – through the medium of their union and their journal, the *Causa Campesina* – the attempts made by the hacienda managements to abandon the traditional paternalistic system that allowed the shepherds to roam freely for one that proposed to convert them into proletarians working for a minimum wage.[17] From Peru, too, we learn from the account of Don Victor, the crafty old leader of peasant 'invasions' of hacienda lands and 'gobernador' of his village, that, when charged with being a member of APRA, the illegal opposition party, he solemnly declared that he had 'no politics'.[18] (But this may, of course, have been a ruse to fool his interrogators.) Sometimes we may trace the transition from the earlier to the later ideology of protest, as in Bolivia where there was a marked contrast between the ideology underlying protest up to the early 1940s, when peasant demands did not go beyond demanding restitution of lost rights or land, and the forward-looking ideology of the Indian serfs who, tutored by leaders like Rojas and Alvarez, aspired after the Congress of 1945 to carry through a total constitutional change.

In Ecuador the transition appears to have been more recent, as Reform, initiated in 1964, proceeded at so slow a pace that it was estimated four years later that it would take another 170 years for all the 'feudal' tenants in the country to be given land. A second Reform Law followed, with the intention of speeding matters up, in 1973. But serfdom and semi-serfdom continued, as is evident from a song composed by members of the Ecuadorian Peasant Federation at the time of a meeting of peasant leaders in 1975. It was clearly not composed by a typical peasant, but the yearning for land and freedom, so long delayed, appears in the following concluding verses:

> We will no longer be serfs,
> there will be no pariahs,
> when the peasantry
> makes an 'Agrarian Reform'.

> The priest from my village
> told me to wait . . .
> But I cannot endure any more,
> I want an 'Agrarian Reform'.[19]

In Mexico the peasants were drawn to Morelos in 1810 – as Russian serfs had been drawn to Pugachev a few years before – by the millenarial hope of a sudden regeneration. There was little sign of this in the revolution of 1910, by which time the peasants had already been drawn into numerous confrontations for immediate ends and looked to Madero to give them simple justice. But belief in the need to return to a better past, to an age when the *haciendado* was less rapacious, certainly persisted. Zapata himself – as no doubt his closest associates – was impelled by an ideology that looked back as well as forward. On the one hand, he always carried with him an image of the Virgin of Guadalupe and wore it emblazoned on his battle-flags as a sign of his deep attachment to tradition. But, on the other, he soon went far beyond the elemental demand for 'justice' and for the restoration of traditional rights to one for a wholesale agrarian reform. We can follow this transition in the few weeks separating a Memorial drawn up by the Zapatists in late September 1911 and the Ayala Plan adopted merely two months later. In the Memorial the main demand is still that 'to the pueblos there be given what in justice they deserve as to lands, timber and water . . .'; while in November, two weeks before the Ayala Plan itself, this early demand had been dropped and replaced by a forward-looking demand that 'there be granted an agrarian law attempting to improve the conditions of the labourer in the field'; whereas both demands appear reunited, alongside several others, in the Plan of Ayala, issued from Zapata's headquarters on 25 November. All this became reformulated, four years later, in a Zapatist draft for an Agrarian Law that went beyond the Ayala provisions and was conceived as a direct ripost, and improvement, to Carranza's 'stolen' reform decree, that began the long legislative process to free the Mexican peasant, of January 1915.[20]

NOTES

1. Eric Hobsbawm, 'Peasant Movements in Colombia', *International Journal of Economic and Social History*, no. 8 (n.d. 1976?), p. 182.

2. In addition, up to the 1940s, banditry has been a frequent phenomenon in the countryside. On occasion it may have served as an adjunct to popular revolt (Pancho Villa, for example, was a former bandit); but where, as often in parts of Bolivia and Colombia, it was an offshoot of a patron-client relationship in which the bandit operated under the protection of a part of the establishment, it appears to have acted as a break rather than as a stimulus to the organization of collective protest. See Linda Lewin, 'The Oligarchical Limitations of Social Banditry in Brazil', *Past and Present*, no. 82 (February 1979), pp. 116–46, esp. 140–6.

3. The seven countries were Argentina, Brazil, Colombia, Chile, Ecuador, Guatemala and Peru. Landsberger (ed.) *Rural Protest*, p. 182.

4. G. Huizer and K. Stavenhagen, 'Peasant Movements and Land Reform in Latin America: Mexico and Bolivia', in Landsberger, *Rural Protest*, pp. 378–9. It was in Ecuador, where peonage still survived in 1975, that the disparities were greatest with 1 per cent of farms holding 57 per cent of all agrarian land (*Journ. of Peasant Studies*, iv (2), January 1977, 226).

5. Huizer and Stavenhagen pp. 379–81; Hobsbawm, pp. 185–6.

6. 'Chispas: From Peasant to "Bandit"', *JPS*, ii (2), January 1974, 245–52.

7. For a good account of the operations of one highly successful and well organized village, see 'The Account of Don Victor', *JPS*, ii (3), April 1975, 355–9.

8. Huizer and Stavenhagen, pp. 380–1, 392–9; also 'Antonio Mamani Alvarez: A Call to Bolivian Indians', *JPS*, iii (3), April 1976, 394–7.

9. Eric Wolf, *Peasant Wars of the Twentieth Century*, New York, 1969, p. 3.

10. Frank Tannenbaum, *The Mexican Agrarian Revolution*, New York, 1928, pp. 165–71; cit. Huizer and Stavenhagen, p. 383.

11. *The New York Times*, 18 March 1919; cit. John Womack, *Zapata and the Mexican Revolution*, London, 1968, p. 321.

12. For this brief account of Zapata's career, see Huizer and Stavenhagen, pp. 382–3; and also Womack, *passim*. According to one author, the Revolution may, by the time of Villa's death (1923), have accounted for as many as 2 million lives. Charles Cumberland, *Mexico: The Struggle for Modernity*, New York, 1968; cit. Wolf, p. 44.

13. Wolf, p. 45.

14. Huizer and Stavenhagen, p. 387.

15. Wolf, p. 37.

16. For a discussion of this point, see H. Landsberger, in *Rural Protest*, pp. 47–51; see also Wolf, loc. cit.

17. 'Peru: Letters from Shepherds' Union Bulletin', *JPS*, 1 (i), October 1973, pp. 112–16.

18. 'The Account of Don Victor', *JPS*, ii (3), April 1975, p. 357.

19. 'The Agrarian Reform', *JPS*, iii (2), January 1976, pp. 225–6.

20. Womack, pp. 393–411.

Part Three

REVOLUTIONS

1

The English Revolution

And now to consider a number of revolutions. Revolutions, apart from their other peculiarities, are notorious as being forcing-grounds of ideology, particularly of popular ideologies of protest. A common feature of the revolutions that I shall be discussing in the next four chapters is that all occurred (with one debatable exception) in a 'pre-industrial' period, when the struggle for power or survival – whether for the control of the state or for more limited objectives – was not confined to two major contestants alone. Admittedly, each of the revolutions to be considered were the battle-grounds of two principal contenders – in all but the last these being (very broadly speaking) the 'rising' bourgeoisie and the established feudal or aristocratic class that it was seeking to displace from the levers of social and political control. But there is more to it than that: in each of these revolutions – but again this does not really apply to the last – there was also an additional popular element that was also struggling for a place in the sun, though it will become evident that this was more conspicuously the case in some examples than in others. In the English revolution of the seventeenth century, there were not only the leaders of Parliament and the New Model Army, the Presbyterians and Independents (all broadly representative of a 'bourgeois' challenge), but also the Levellers, Diggers and lower-class sectaries, who offered some sort of challenge in the name of other, 'lower', social groups. In America, besides the Southern planters and the Boston merchants and Sons of Liberty, there were also the sailors and mechanics, the Jack Tars and White Oaks whose challenge in this case was brief and relatively muted. In France, in 1789, the official Third Estate – the bourgeoisie and its liberal-aristocratic allies – had to face a far more sustained challenge than their opposite numbers in England and America from the peasants and urban *sans-culottes*. And similar lower-class challengers to purely bourgeois aspirations appeared in the French Revolutions of the nineteenth century, as they also appeared in the German, the Austrian, the Italian and other revolutionary outbreaks in the 'year of revolutions', 1848. So, however 'bourgeois' these revolutions may have been, they were also the seed-bed for a challenge 'from below', opening other perspectives and presenting a kind of 'revolution within the revolution' (though not quite in the sense intended by Régis Debray),[1] whose nature varied from one to the other. But, in each case, the challenge, though posing a problem for the principal revolutionaries, was not entirely unwelcome; for without the support of their lower-class partners in the villages and streets, how could they have toppled Charles I or Louis XVI from their thrones, overthrown a Bastille or a feudal system, or driven a Charles X, a Louis Philippe or a Metternich into exile? Yet, once these tasks were completed, there soon came a parting of the ways: Cromwell gave short shrift to the Levellers, who offered the only serious challenge, soon after the execution of Charles; the Jacobins and *sans-culottes* ended their alliance once Louis was dead and the old aristocracy silenced; and, in the French revolution of 1848, the partnership of 'blouse' and 'redingote' served well enough to exile Louis Philippe and institute the Republic; but, before that republic could be given a more 'democratic' form, the middle and lower-class allies of February fought it out to a bloody finish in June. And, of course, subsuming and transcending these events, there was always a battle of ideas.[2]

But, clearly, it is not enough to present the problem in such general terms. Each revolution, while sharing with others such common features, has a face of its own and must be treated in its own right in addition. To arrive at these specifics of revolutions – notably as they relate to popular ideology – we have to begin to take note of such questions as the society within which the revolution took place; the prevailing ideology of both the established class and the principal contenders for power on the eve of revolution; and the 'inherent' ideas of the 'popular' classes – the workers, smallholders and peasants – before the revolution began. And once the revolution starts, or is about to start, we must go on to consider the means whereby the new, 'derived', ideas were transmitted to the lower classes, the stages of that transmission, and the exact nature of the new popular ideology that emerged after the blending of the old and new.

And, finally, we must consider the part played by popular ideology in the revolution; and, if we are able to do so, consider its fate once the revolution – or, at least, the 'popular' phase of the revolution – was over. All this might seem fairly obvious and barely worth the emphasis I am giving it, were it not for a certain fashion – more common in North America than in England and France – to apply ready-made models to revolutionary situations and to leave the specifics to look after themselves.

To come, then, to the main subject of this chapter, the English revolution of the seventeenth century. The system of government at the time was that of the early Stuarts, a developing despotism though not comparable in unchallenged sovereignty to that of the absolute monarchy being developed in France. In England, sovereignty was shared, though to a diminishing degree, by the Parliament at Westminster, representing the landed classes and larger merchants and, more significantly, in the counties, where the large estates of the aristocracy and their control of the justices of the peace served as a weighty balance to the authority of the Crown. Society itself was aristocratic in the sense that it was dominated by the large land-owners who, though serfdom had been abolished a century before, retained an almost feudal control of their tenants and retainers. (This will appear in the comparative ease with which the landowners on both sides of the Civil War will be able to recruit their armies.) The gentry were by tradition a junior branch of the aristocracy, yet their increasing involvement in trade brought them ever closer to the merchant class. The 'middle sort of people' (as both contemporaries and historians have found it convenient to call them) were the yeomanry, farmers, freeholders and clothiers of the countryside and the 'mechanical men', the shopkeepers, master craftsmen and their apprentices in the towns; and, at the base of the social pyramid were the 'inferior people' – the common peasants and cottagers, the journeymen, servants and so-called 'rabble' or 'rude rascals' of the towns. And interspersed among these lower classes were others less stable and harder to categorize – the uprooted 'masterless men' described by Christopher Hill in his *World Turned Upside Down*.[3]

Of these classes and groups, as in all revolutions, some were to prove significantly more 'revolutionary' than others. When it came to the point, most of the aristocrats found that it accorded best with their interests – and, maybe too, with their traditions – to support the King, while about a third, for a variety of reasons, rallied to Parliament. The gentry were also divided in similar proportions, though in this case loyalties were reversed; and, in their case too, divisions tended to respond to regional boundaries, those of the North and West (with notable exceptions, as we shall see) opting for the King and those of the South and East rallying to Parliament. The merchants – particularly those of the ports and manufacturing towns – joined Parliament. Of the 'inferior' and 'middle' sort of people, the 'rabble' or 'rascality' (as often in revolutions) played little or no part at all, except perhaps as vociferous bystanders who echoed the slogans of others. The small peasants and journeymen played an important role in the early affrays; but as the revolution developed into a protracted civil war, it was the 'middle sort of men' – the farmers, craftsmen and the like – that, together with the 'godly people', were the most persistent revolutionaries of all.[4] These, once the shooting started, would be the real shock-troops of revolution, much as the Parisian *sans-culottes* (though of a somewhat different social composition) would be in the revolution in France in 1789.

What was the ideology of these contending classes? (It must be understood, of course, that it did not remain static and that the ideologies of both 'upper', 'middle' and 'lower'-class revolutionaries changed as the revolution progressed or declined.) The dominant ideology of revolution was provided by the merchants and gentry, who, in the counties and towns, as well as in Parliament itself, set the revolution going and provided its leaders. It was composed of two elements, the one secular and the other religious, with a considerable overlap between the two. The secular element was concerned with the protection of property, with trade, and the 'liberties' of Parliament against the encroachments and 'despotism' of the King and his principal ministers, Archbishop Laud and the Earl of Strafford. Such ideas derived from earlier struggles over the Common Law and Magna Carta, seen as bastions of Parliament's liberties against the claims of royal Divine Right and, more generally, from the whole tradition of the 'Norman Yoke'. The religious ideology had a shorter history, being based on the teachings of Luther and Calvin (though appreciably more on the latter than the former) as interpreted by generations of Puritan divines. But the Puritans, as Hill and others have argued, were as much outraged by the inroads of royal 'despotism', which threatened their liberties, as by the 'popish' practices and innovations of Archbishop Laud. This explains, of course, why Laud and Strafford, the twin agents of 'popery' and 'repression', became the principal targets of popular fury even before the Civil War began. Broadly, we may say that this dominant ideology of revolution, though emanating in the first place from the merchants and gentry and from the Puritan clergy whose sermons they attended, permeated widely among the 'middle' and 'inferior' sort of people and tended to become the ideology of all.

But these latter groups also came into the revolution with an ideology of their own. Its nature depended, not unnaturally, on the occupations and classes to which they belonged. By far the largest class was that formed by the small farmers, freeholders and poor peasants (whether copyholders, tenants, or simple labourers). For some years before the revolution started, the small proprietors' fortunes had been steadily declining. This took a variety of forms: of rising fines on estates of inheritance, the forcible exchange of copyhold for leasehold tenancies, 'rack-renting', massive evictions by lords for non-payment of rents or fines, or – a feature of a recent 'feudal reaction' – the exaction of long-forgotten fines and obligations, whose harmful effects were compounded by a succession of bad harvests and a rapid growth of the rural population. In addition, lords were enclosing wastes and commons and, with the collaboration of the Crown, draining marshes and fens – as in Somerset and Lincoln – to the injury of the people's common rights. To defend themselves the peasants resorted, in the first place, to litigation and, when that failed, to direct action; and the decade before the revolution broke out witnessed a considerable peasant revolt levelled against enclosures, dykes and drainage works, much to the consternation of the landlords and government, particularly when juries refused to convict arrested offenders and the Commons, anxious not to forfeit the freeholders' votes, chose to conciliate rather than to repress. Through this experience, the peasants added to their traditional concern for their right of possession of land and the free use of commons a new political awareness, directed against the House of Lords and, increasingly as the political crisis developed, against the King himself.[5]

Meanwhile, the craftsmen and other small producers of both towns and countryside had problems of their own. In industry, the basic conflict was not one between masters and workmen – this belonged to the future – but between craftsmen and merchants; and the issues that divided them were most commonly the price and quality of what the craftsman produced. The principal industry in England at this time was the manufacture of cloth, whose sale on foreign markets was largely controlled by monopoly companies of which the largest was that of the Merchant Adventurers. The long depression in the trade led to bitter disputes between the clothiers and provincial merchants on the one side and the great companies on the other for a share in a dwindling market, with the dice loaded increasingly against the provincials. The economic struggle was further embittered by the political struggle within the chartered towns over municipal government, in which the privileges of the oligarchies formed by wealthy merchants (as in the City of London) were contested by the general body of craftsmen, supported by the shopkeepers and smaller merchants. So these opponents of oligarchy were naturally drawn towards Parliament for protection, and even before the revolution began, Manning quotes numerous petitions of citizens of the 'middle' sort, that express their resentment at the flouting of ancient rights and demand the restoration of the traditional right to vote.[6] The 'lower' sort of people had, of course, even more pressing concerns; and we are told that the London crowds demonstrating against Strafford in May 1641 accompanied their cry for 'Justice' with the older and more traditional cry for 'Bread'.[7]

But, in addition, common to all groups (but, no doubt, with significant exceptions in the North) was the general concern for the true Faith, the Protestant religion as understood by the Puritan preachers. Long experience and folk-memory of the persecutions of Bloody Mary and the ambitions of Philip of Spain had taught them that 'Popery' meant enslavement and 'wooden shoes' and was the main enemy of English 'liberties'.

This was part of the people's traditional ideology which they brought with them into the revolution. In this regard, it did not require the imposition of new ideas to give them a wider intellectual experience. But, even so, it did need the sermons of the preachers, the panics engendered by the Scottish and Irish wars, the economic crisis and the 'tyranny' of Charles to stoke up the fires anew, to give the old popish enemy an even more villainous image, and lend a keener edge to popular fears.

But new ideas were also expounded from the pulpit, the main medium for their communication particularly for those unable to read: ideas concerning the new divisions within the Protestant Church; the rights of Parliament to resist oppression, to resort to arms against their King and, later, to behead him. An alternative means of communication was provided by itinerant craftsmen, 'masterless men' that roamed from village to village.[8] Later, when political debate became more heated among the victors as the Civil War drew to a close, the main forum for discussion and the exchange and indoctrination of ideas was undoubtedly the Army, as on the occasion of the famous Putney debates of 1647. In addition, there were, of course, also the newspapers and pamphlets that proliferated during the early years of revolution when the Press was free and carried shortened versions of the speeches of the leaders for those who could read them or were in a position to hear them read. It is evident that such propaganda was more readily acceptable to some groups than to others: to some it set political goals and gave a stimulus to action; others, to whom it brought no solutions to present ills, it left comparatively cold. To see how the different groups *in fact* reacted to the revolution, whether prompted by old experience or new propaganda, it may be useful to divide the active period of revolution – that is, the period during which the popular element may be said to have been politically engaged – into three: first, the years 1640–42, from the first meetings of the Long Parliament to the outbreak of civil war; second, the years of civil war and Charles's execution (autumn 1642 to January 1649); and, third, the muting of political debate that followed Charles's death (1649–53).

The most striking feature of the first period, which centred around the political struggle between King and Parliament at

Westminster, was the continual tumults in the streets of London, directed in turn against Strafford, the Church of England Bishops, and the 'Popish' Lords; these popular activities served the interests of the radical group in Parliament and the religious 'separatists' and led to the execution of Strafford in May 1641. The rioters, though described by unsympathetic contemporaries as a 'rude rabble', 'inferior persons' or 'round-headed dogs', were more often craftsmen and apprentices (themselves usually the sons of men of 'good rank') rather than servants, beggars or common 'mob'. But these political demonstrations generally had economic undertones: bread was scarce and manufacture was at a low ebb. The same mixture of political and economic motivation among the crowds appeared when the agitation spread – after the King's attempt to arrest the Five Members in Parliament in January 1642 – to Kent, Sussex, Northampton and, particularly, to the clothing-manufacturing districts of Essex and Suffolk. These, which continued for long to be among the centres most committed to the cause of Parliament, were suffering an acute economic depression.

When – to move on to the second phase – the Civil War started in the late summer of 1642, there were widespread popular insurrections, erupting almost spontaneously in the northern and eastern counties; they invoked the name of Parliament and were directed against 'papists', 'malignants' and 'cavaliers'. Both men and women, of both the 'middle' and 'inferior' sort, took part; but it was observed that even in the urban outbreaks the main participants were peasants, who marched in from their villages to aid the townsmen, often armed with only clubs and scythes.[9] In the South, the peasants took advantage of the unsettled conditions to strike back at their landlords, assaulting their deer parks and refusing to pay rent. So, in a sense, in these parts at least, the peasant rebellion was a continuation of what had been started before in a more muted form rather than anything related directly to the struggle between King and Parliament.[10] Moreover, the spontaneous popular risings in support of Parliament did not long outlast the first year of civil war: once the initial 'papist' scare was over (or at least removed from their district), the harvest appeared to beckon and the peasants were anxious to return to their fields. And, from this stage, too, 'the inferior sort' – the poorer peasants and townsmen – began to lose their zeal for Parliament, as it appeared to offer no solution for their problems.[11]

But most farmers and craftsmen – those of 'the middle sort' – remained in the fight and many came to serve in the New Model Army, alongside Cromwell's 'plain russet-coated captain', at the end of 1644. The 'godly men', too, continued as stalwart supporters of Parliament; and they also appear to have been largely found among the 'middle' ranks of the population. And it was from these 'middling' strata, rather than from the working people as a whole, that a new popular ideology of revolution, a blend of new and old elements, now began to emerge. It had two main strains, a secular and a 'godly', though these, for reasons already explained, were inevitably confused. The more secular strain is that associated with the Levellers and Diggers, both of whom, though their programmes differed widely, offered political and social solutions for earthly ills. They emerged from the furious debates between Army officers (favouring the larger merchants and owners of estates) and 'Agitators', representing the Army rank and file, staged at Putney in 1647. Some Levellers at first called for equality of property, thus meriting the label of 'leveller' applied to them by their critics. But, as the debates continued, the main group of Levellers (including John Lilburne, their chief spokesman) rejected collectivist ideas; but they went on, in their petitions and manifestoes, to condemn monopoly, to call for the abolition of tithe (though with compensation for owners) and imprisonment for debt, for legal reform and for an end to the enclosure of commons and wastes. So they had a social policy of considerable scope and one calculated to find support among the small propertied classes, though it fell far short of the more radical aspiration of the unpropertied poor – the servants, paupers, labourers and economically unfree.

Such groups, in fact, the main group of Levellers (the 'constitutional' Levellers) omitted not only from their social programme but from their constitutional programme as well. A great deal of ink has been used on the vexed question: how far did the Levellers go along the road to democracy? In the Putney debates there were some, like the radical Colonel Rainborough, who appeared to favour an extension of the suffrage to include

all adult males ('the smallest he that is in England' among them).
But the eventual decision of Lilburne and his associates, though
the formulations often varied, was to settle for something like a
household vote, but excluding not only servants and beggars
but all men working for wages.[12] These groups, then, insofar as
they refused to accept their lot, had to look for champions in
other quarters. These appeared, briefly, in the movement of
Diggers, or True Levellers, who preached the forcible
occupation of wastelands and commons by the landless poor, as
was first put into practice on St George's Hill, near Cobham in
Surrey, in April 1649. A dozen other Digger colonies followed,
mainly in southern and central England, in the next two years;
their principal spokesman was Gerrard Winstanley, who not
only formulated solutions for agrarian ills but looked forward
to a cooperative Commonwealth of the future in which all
property should be held in common.[13] Winstanley's work has
survived to enrich other speculations on the perfect society; but
the Diggers' movement was shortlived, not least because it
evoked little sympathy among the freeholders, yeomen and
citizens of 'the middle sort' for whom the main body of Levellers
spoke. Which is not surprising, as their interests as small
proprietors stood in the way and made them no more willing to
open the commons to an invasion by the rural poor than the
gentry and lords. But even before the Diggers went down, the
Levellers' political movement had been suppressed, after an
attempt to raise mutinies in the army, in May 1649.

It has been suggested that the 'constitutional' Levellers,
because of their compromises and hesitations to upset the
propertied classes, were not in fundamental disagreement with
the type of capitalist society that was emerging from the English
revolution.[14] Taken without qualification it appears a harsh
judgment, as the Levellers' attempt to create a democracy of
small producers was an attempt that (the Ancient Greeks
notwithstanding) had never been made before and would not be
made again until the revolution in France a century and a half
later. Yet it is true that the Levellers spoke for a class that hoped
to extend its properties within an acquisitive society and had,
therefore, no intention, once their 'salad-days' were over, of
'turning the world upside down'. But this, according to Hill, is

precisely what the radical religious sects – the Ranters, Seekers and Quakers – intended to do.

Like Winstanley, with whom these sects had a certain intellectual affinity, they rejected Sin and Hell and the Protestant Ethic that was central to traditional Calvinist teaching. The most extreme of them, the Ranters, turned the theological wheel full circle by rejecting God and immortality. 'All (is) made by Nature', proclaimed a Ranter Christmas card that Hill quotes. 'They prate of God', it continues, 'there's no such bugbear'.[15] In gross violation of Calvinist ethics, sexual freedom became a linch-pin of Ranter philosophy. One of their spokesmen, Abiezer Coppe, at one time preached that 'adultery, fornication and uncleanness is no sin', and that 'community of wives is lawful'; and Lawrence Clarkson, a one-time Baptist turned Ranter, believed that 'No man could be freed from sin, till he had acted that so-called sin as no sin. . . . Till you can lie with all women as one woman, and not judge it sin, you can do nothing but sin.'[16] This attempted 'sexual revolution' of the 1650s, Hill suggests, is an interesting foretaste of certain aspects of the 'counter-culture' of the 1960s. But a more relevant question in the present context is, what significance did it have for the popular protest – the 'revolution within the revolution' – of the revolutionaries of seventeenth-century England? There certainly was a connection between some of the sectaries and the radical political movement – through Winstanley, for example; and one of their leaders, James Nayler, a Quaker with strong Ranter and 'levelling' leanings, wrote in 1654, in a paper denouncing the rich, that God 'made all men of one mould and one blood to dwell on the face of the earth'.[17] It also appears that the Ranters found recruits in London and the Army among apprentices and young people.[18] So there may have been something of a 'generation gap' between supporters and opponents of the sects. Hill also suggests, without spelling it out, that the Ranters and Seekers had a particular message for the 'masterless men' who resented authority; and it has even been suggested (though not by Hill) that the Ranters, in particular, had a 'proletarian' appeal. It may be so though it would be hard to prove. If it were so and if these notions may with justice be considered a part of the ideology of the young and the poor, we still have to ask whether it be as protest or as compensation for what the Revolution failed to provide. It is true enough that to the Englishman of the seventeenth century religion, including its most unorthodox manifestations, could be a vital weapon in the armoury of protest; and where would John Lilburne, or Cromwell's 'plain russet-coated captain', or even Cromwell himself, have been without it? But the despairing cries and gestures of the sectaries look more like a retreat than a call to advance to a better future. In this respect, they may have served a role similar to that of the evangelical sects in nineteenth-century Britain who offered the one-time labour militants that joined them compensation for temporal defeats.[19] And, as evidence to support this view, Hill tells us that several of the best-known Seekers had previously had close radical connections and had been disappointed, if not demoralized, by the army's failure to create a democratic society after 1647;[20] and it is certainly significant that the Ranters and Seekers and others only came to flourish in the early 1650s – that is, after the Levellers, the most consistent champions of an egalitarian society, had been reduced to virtual silence.

So, in terms of popular protest, we are left with the Levellers and Diggers. Of these the Diggers have left a considerable literature but they have left no mark on the course of history; the Levellers alone have done so. Admittedly, they failed to win their grand objective of a society of small producers; yet they won, temporarily at least, the Republic they had worked for. They also left a legacy that it is hard to pin down exactly, though some of their democratic ideas were carried with the 'Commonwealthmen' to the United States;[21] and were it not for the black-out in popular activity in England after Sedgemoor (1685) it would be easier to chart more exactly the influence they had on the popular-democratic movement, no longer the particular province of the 'middle sort' of men, that started up again in the middle decades of the eighteenth century in England. In that sense, their ideas, though driven underground during the Restoration, surfaced a century later; and Hill quotes the words of an enemy of the Army radicals, Clement Walker, which may serve as an epitaph:

They have cast all the mysteries and secrets of government . . .

before the vulgar . . . , and have taught both the soldiery and people to look so far into them as to ravel back all governments to the first principles of nature. . . . They have made the people thereby so curious and so arrogant that they will never find humility enough to submit to a civil rule.[22]

NOTES

1. Régis Debray, *Revolution within the Revolution?*, New York/London, 1967.
2. For an elaboration of this theme, see G. Rudé, 'Revolution and Popular Ideology', in M. Allain and G. R. Conrad (eds), *France and North America: The Revolutionary Experience*, Lafayette, Louisiana, 1974, pp. 142–58.
3. Christopher Hill, *The World Turned Upside Down*, London/New York, 1972, pp. 32–45.
4. See Brian Manning, *The English People and the English Revolution*, Peregrine, 1978, esp. pp. 258–65.
5. Manning, pp. 128–54.
6. ibid., pp. 155–77.
7. ibid., pp. 115.
8. Hill, pp. 36–7.
9. Manning, pp. 186, 189, 222, 229.
10. ibid., pp. 202–15. In Manning's own words: 'The hunting of lords and deer in the late summer and autumn of 1642 was only loosely connected with the challenge of parliament to the king; the rioters often had little sympathy with parliament or interest in the disputes between the king and the two houses' (p. 211).
11. Manning, pp. 186, 189, 222, 229.
12. For recent interpretations, see C. B. Macpherson, *The Political Theory of Possessive Individualism*, Oxford, 1962; Manning, pp. 308–40; Hill, pp. 86–120.
13. For Winstanley, see Hill, pp. 86–99, 267–75; and C. Hill (ed.) *Winstanley. The Law of Freedom and other Writings*, London, 1973.
14. Hill, *The World Turned Upside Down*, p. 99.
15. ibid., p. 148.
16. ibid., p. 254.
17. ibid., p. 199.
18. ibid., pp. 152–3.
19. For evidence of this view, see E. P. Thompson, *The Making of the English Working Class*, London, 1962, pp. 427–9. E. J. Hobsbawm, *Labouring Men*, New York, 1965, pp. 22–33; and Hobsbawm and Rudé, *Captain Swing*, London, 1969, pp. 288–91.
20. Hill, p. 154.
21. Caroline Robbins, *The Eighteenth-Century Commonwealth*, Cambridge, Mass., 1959.
22. Cit. Hill, p. 58.

2

The American Revolution

American society of the 1760s differed in several respects from England's a century before. For one thing, there was in America no significant trace of a feudal system; such survivals had not been among those that accompanied the settlers to the new Continent in the early seventeenth century, nor did the conditions in which they found themselves on the other side of the Atlantic tend to reproduce them. There was no hereditary peerage, and there were no manorial lords of the 'bastard-feudal' kind that still survived in England when the Civil War broke out; and the smallholders and farmers, though they still had problems with land and tenures, bore little resemblance to the peasantry which, on the Continent of Europe, continued into the nineteenth, or even twentieth, century. But, on the other hand, a considerable part of the American economy, though never feudal in the European sense, was worked by the chattle-labour of 500,000 blacks and the social relations binding slaves to slave-owners in the cotton and tobacco plantations of the South, although their origins went back to the slave trade of European nations – France and Britain, in particular – had no equivalent – even allowing for pockets of slavery in Catherine's Russia – in the states of Europe.

In some important respects, however, there were close similarities between English and American society at the end of the Seven Years' War. One was, of course, religion, for the Puritan strain in a great deal of American political thinking was, as is well known, an offshoot of the English. In both countries, the gentry, through its ownership of land, played a predominant social and political role; and, in both, capitalism was still at the mercantile stage and it was merchants (rather than manufacturers) who controlled the affairs of industry and trade. Yet even here there were significant differences. One was that whereas London, Britain's largest port and capital city, had a mid-century population of nearly 700,000, Philadelphia, the largest town and port in the Thirteen Colonies, had a population of 25,000. This in itself complicates the problem of attempting to compare the urban life and activities of the two communities. The other major difference, of course – and this was fundamental – was that whereas British merchants and gentry could expect their Parliament and government to give careful consideration to their wishes, the Americans, having no central representative institutions of their own, had their fortunes decided by others. In consequence, the American Revolution when it came – in 1765 or in 1776, according to the historians' fancy – was bound to have as its primary aim to set up a Parliament of the colonists' own choice and to pose the question of national sovereignty and of loosening or breaking such ties as stood in the way.

But though this was bound to be the primary aim, and one shared with varying degrees of enthusiasm by all classes (though, paradoxically, rather less by those who really needed freedom – the slaves),[1] the Americans, like the English or the French, were divided among themselves and there was therefore bound to be a social conflict as well that both preceded the struggle for national independence and merged with or ran parallel to it when the Revolution broke out. Historians have naturally disagreed about the importance of this second conflict, but of its existence there can be no doubt whatever. Its pattern and the issues raised naturally differed between the towns and countryside. In the latter there were landlords on the one side and small farmers and smallholders on the other; and the issue that brought them into conflict was most frequently the tenure or ownership of land (and not the shortage of food, as so often in contemporary Europe). In the larger towns (Philadelphia, Boston, Charleston and New York) on the one hand were the wealthy merchants, becoming richer and more powerful as the century went on and, on the other, the 'mechanics' (the more prosperous artisans), the lesser craftsmen and labourers, for whom good wages and conditions of work and trade were matters of prime importance. The heart of the matter was the increasing concentration of wealth in ever fewer hands in America's principal towns. After studying this question with the aid of tax rolls and probate records, Gary Nash, one of a group of young radical historians, writes:

By the early 1770s the top 5 percent of Boston's taxpayers controlled 49 percent of the taxable assets of the community, whereas they had held only 30 percent in 1687. In Philadelphia the top twentieth increased its share of wealth from 33 to 55 percent between 1693 and 1774. Those in the lower half of society, who in Boston in 1687 had commanded 9 percent of the taxable wealth, were left collectively with a mere 5 percent in 1771. In Philadelphia, those in the lower half of the wealth spectrum saw their share of wealth drop from 10·1 to 3·3 percent in the same period.[2]

He illustrates further, from the two poles within 'popular' society, 'the crumbling of middle-class economic security' and the remarkable increase in per capita expenditure on poor relief – doubling in Boston between 1740 and 1760 and doubling again before the end of the colonial period, while in New York the incidence of poverty increased four times over between 1750 and 1775.[3]

Such being the problems, it is hardly surprising that, particularly at times of economic crisis, as in the early 1760s and 1770s, there should have been a popular response in the form of riots and uprisings. These took place intermittently in both towns and countryside. On the land, there were three main outbreaks: the land riots in New Jersey in the 1740s; the Hudson Valley tenant disturbances of the 1750s and 1760s; and the insurgency in north-eastern New York that, starting in 1764, only ended after the War began, with the creation of the break-away state of Vermont in 1777. In each case the issue was not so much one of individual tenure as of the conditions of tenancy attaching to whole rural communities. In consequence, these movements tended to be protracted rather than short or sudden outbreaks. They also tended to be better organized than urban riots, though less so in the Hudson Valley, where the movement occurred in two stages of which the second stage (that of 1766) was the better organized and more structured of the two. At that time they formally elected a leader, William Prendergast, a Dutchess county farmer, and a committee of twelve, and they formed militia companies with elected captains to command them. The insurgents in New Jersey went further: they appointed a coordinating committee even before the outbreak began, divided themselves into wards, and raised taxes and set up their own law courts in the course of the dispute. The New York rebels, in the early 1770s, formed a military force called the Green Mountain Boys whom it would have needed the British Army (by now engaged on other duties) to disperse.[4]

In the towns, popular outbreaks were naturally more varied and were inclined to be more spontaneous. They also tended to become more involved with politics (and certainly at an earlier stage) than those in England. Pauline Maier has argued that many eighteenth-century riots in America, whether rural or urban, were of a vigilante kind and that through them the common people sought to defend the interests of their communities when the lawful authorities failed to do so; and she cites among her examples the frequent intervention of the Boston 'mob' to restrict bawdy houses and to keep foodstuffs in the colony in times of shortage.[5] Other historians – notably Gary Nash, Edward Countryman and Dirk Hoerder (all contributors to Alfred Young's 'radical' volume) – have disputed the point and substituted the notion of 'class' for that of 'community'. They have insisted that, after the 1730s at least, popular outbreaks in America, like those in Europe, were typically made in response to worsening economic conditions, involving unemployment and rising prices, and that, even before the middle of the century, urban riots had begun to assume a political complexion that accorded with the class needs of both the 'middling' and poorer groups of citizens. At Boston, in one of the major riots of the first half of the century, in 1737, rioters, inflamed by the control of the public market in the interests of the larger merchants, destroyed the market in Dock Square, the attack being accompanied by much 'murmuring agt the Government & the rich . . .'.[6] Nash argues that the beginnings of a popular political awakening were hastened by the religious 'awakening' brought into the streets of Boston and Philadelphia by George Whitefield and fellow-revivalists in 1739 and 1741, and by an itinerant preacher, James Davenport, who followed them with a blatantly radical message addressed to the poorer classes that caused considerable concern among conservative citizens. Popular radicalism developed further through the Boston impressment riot of 1747 which, nearly two decades before the Stamp Act riots, brought the crowd into confrontation with Thomas Hutchinson, a wealthy merchant and friend of government, who was later to become lieutenant governor, president of the council and chief justice of the colony. In the protracted campaign that followed, in which Hutchinson gained increasing unpopularity, the craftsmen and labourers found leadership and received further

political instruction from a group of radical merchants
including James Otis and Samuel Adams.[7]

The Stamp Act riots of 1765 marked a new development. For
one thing, they marked the point from which the Americans'
'resistance' (Pauline Maier's term) to the British authorities
became continuous until the breaking-off of relations and war
in 1776. For another, they marked the point at which the urban
crowds of labourers, mechanics and sailors, whether taking the
initiative themselves or following that of the middle-class
'patriots', began to appear to their former middle-class leaders
as almost as great a menace as their British oppressors. The best-
known example of this sort of combined initiative (and of the
mixed ideology that lay behind it) is perhaps that of the Boston
events of August 1765, when the Whig leaders known as the
Loyal Nine organized the opposition to the new duties being
levied by the British. They called upon the master craftsmen
from the city's North and South end to settle their traditional
quarrel over the annual Pope's Day celebrations and, drawing
on their long experience, march in serried ranks in a peaceful
demonstration. As a symbolic act of resistance, they were
encouraged to carry effigies of the stamp officials and were even
allowed to pull down a half-completed building belonging to
Andrew Oliver, a stamp master. But, at this point, the crowd took
over and, flouting the leaders' directions, converted the peaceful
demonstration into a violent assault on the mansions of both
Oliver and Hutchinson. Similar events in New York led to an
even more violent result. One outcome was that the Stamp Act
was repealed; but another result, even more significant, was that
the riots drove a wedge between the lower-class crowds and their
middle-class leaders; and, as General Gage, the British
commander-in-chief, observed in looking back on the event,
'. . . there has been so much Pain taken since to prevent
Insurrections of the People as before to excite them'. So from
now on – through the Townshend duties and non-importation,
the *Liberty* affair and anti-impressment, the Boston 'Massacre'
and the Tea Party – relations between the crowd and Whig or
liberal leaders remained distinctly cool; and often, as over
impressment, the sailors, labourers and craftsmen were left to
fend for themselves. After 1774, with the British military
occupation in support of 'coercion', the Boston crowd became
muted; and Boston 'patriots' were left to contend with a more

structured, less violent, popular radicalism to take its place.[8]

Philadelphia, America's largest city and busiest port, had a greater diversity of population and of crafts than either Boston or New York. Like Boston, its artisans (both 'mechanics' and 'inferior' craftsmen) and labourers had a long history of fighting poverty, unemployment and rising prices, and (as befitted a city with a rapid industrial growth) its mechanics, in particular, had, by the early 1760s, become 'a self-conscious political group with its own organization and demands'.[9] The first political meeting confined to mechanics took place in 1770; and, two years later, master craftsmen founded a Patriotic Society of its own to promote its own candidates and policies. Besides, by the time of Thomas Paine's arrival in the city (1774), a militia had been created that was recruited largely among the artisans and labourers, electing their own officers from among merchants, and, like the New Model Army in Cromwell's day, began to provide a 'school of political democracy' on the eve of the Revolution. It was, in fact, no coincidence that it was at Philadelphia, where popular radicalism reached its highest point before the War of Independence, that Paine chose to settle when he came to America in 1774 and that it was there that he wrote his great pamphlet *Common Sense* less than two years later.[10]

Before we consider how popular ideology developed, we must consider briefly the set of ideas that inspired the upper-class 'patriots' – the gentry and merchants – and brought them through 'resistance' to the fatal step of revolution. The old thesis advanced by Charles Beard and the 'progressives', that the Revolution could be largely explained in terms of a conflict of economic interests has now been largely discarded by both liberal and radical historians. The most popular liberal alternative has been that put forward by Bernard Baylin from the mid-1960s on. This is broadly that, while the clash of economic interest could not be discounted, the colonists, who inherited an English tradition of resistance to 'tyranny' and arbitrary rule, became convinced after 1763 that the English Government intended to impose on America shackles similar to those that the English themselves had experienced under the Stuarts a century before. Thus was born the notion of a 'conspiracy against liberty'; and it was a growing belief in the existence of this 'conspiracy' that, 'above all else, . . . propelled [the colonists] into Revolution'.[11] And, as a corollary, Baylin and his school have argued that, as the masses in America were not impoverished (as their French counterparts were to be in 1789), nor suffering from undue deprivation, it must be assumed that, through the Stamp Act crisis and the coercive measures taken against Boston, they came to share the ideology of the merchants and gentry.

The contributors to Young's *Explorations* have generally dissented from this view, believing that the 'lower' order of citizens had ideological impulses of their own. Among them, Joseph Ernst asks the highly pertinent question, 'Which Americans, or groups of Americans, subscribe to which interpretations, and why?' And he goes on to argue that there were really three types of ideology, reflecting the interests of different social groups. In the first place, there was the ideology 'from the top' of the Baylin kind, which centred on constitutional principle and was therefore peculiar to the gentry and other groups concerned with government and able to comprehend and liable to respond to philosophical abstractions. Secondly, there was the more down-to-earth ideology of practical men – merchants and mechanics – who might unite in common opposition to the economic consequences of the 'imperial system', yet be divided over the best means to remove it, involving such immediate questions as 'non-importation' or protection of domestic industry. And, thirdly, there was the less sophisticated ideology – the 'mentality' or 'curbside ideology' – of the urban poor, the jobless and hungry, which (he insists) needs to be distinguished from the ideology of the 'mechanic and labouring classes'.[12]

More emphasis is given to the ideology of the lower classes – whether mechanics or labouring poor – by Baylin's other critics in this volume – Nash, Hoerder, Foner, Countryman; and it is only through such contributions as theirs (and Jesse Lemisch should not be omitted) that we can begin to trace the development of a popular revolutionary conscience through its various stages: from the purely 'inherent' and traditional beliefs infusing the earlier riots to political involvement and commitment to revolution. We can, in fact, follow this evolution by returning to the evidence that was cited before. First, the earlier decades of largely independent activity over food prices and unemployment, and even of the crowd's activity as an easily tolerated communal watchdog (as insisted by Pauline Maier); at this stage popular rioting appears to have been inspired by traditional notions of justice or social propriety; that is, with no or little intrusion of political and ideological guidance from other groups. From the mid-century the scene changes and, as best illustrated by the example of Boston, there was a short period of perhaps a dozen years during which a new political radicalism emerged, bringing the craftsmen and labourers into alliance with a radical middle-class group, in the course of which the popular and 'middling' elements combined against wealthy merchants and conservative aspirants to high office like Thomas Hutchinson. At this stage, the target of popular hostility was more often the enemy within in the shape of the wealthy merchant than the imperial enemy without. Yet there was never a neat line of separation between the two and hostility to England could quite easily arise among the poorer classes before the new policy of taxing the colonies was proclaimed at Westminster in 1763. A long-standing grievance of Bostonians was their frequent exposure to impressment into the Royal Navy; and, on one such occasion, in 1747, crowds reacted vigorously by taking possession of the town and besieging the Governor in his mansion. And it certainly added little to Hutchinson's future popularity that he made himself conspicuous as a public champion of the Governor's policy.[13]

Yet, to repeat what we said before, the Stamp Act crisis of 1765 was the decisive turning point, as the popular movement now merged with that of the middle-class 'patriots' with Britain becoming the major enemy of both. One aspect of this transition, in terms of ideology, is that described by Alfred Young in his study of the traditional Pope's Day ritual in Boston: at about this time (he relates) the old Protestant Pope-burning ceremony, dating from the days of Guy Fawkes, was converted into the burning in effigy (another old English custom) of His Majesty's Ministers.[14] The other, more tangible, aspect was revealed in the events of August 1765, when (it will be remembered) the middle-class 'patriots' of the Loyal Nine, to denote their displeasure with Britain's policies, called on the city's craftsmen to march in a peaceful procession. The common people, however, who harboured longer and more varied grievances, while responding to the 'patriots' call, also took the occasion to avenge ancient wrongs by destroying the properties of two old enemies and threatening to destroy a dozen more. Thus the ideology of the crowd, though enriched and given a more precise focus by the 'patriotic' Whigs, also drew on longer traditions and experience of its own.[15]

In Philadelphia, as we saw, popular radicalism took shape earlier and reached a higher stage of maturity before the War of Independence broke out. But how long did this popular radicalism continue to run in harness with that of the middle-class 'patriots'; and, whether in alliance with the 'patriots' or not, did it continue its independent existence after the War broke out? The evidence provided by historians on this point is remarkably thin. In Boston, as we have seen, the crowd ceased its operations after 1774, largely because of the presence of troops but also, maybe, because that official toleration of the crowd that Pauline Maier writes about, had by now worn very thin indeed. In Philadelphia, where popular radicalism certainly continued, it had become directed into the more durable channels of political and military organization, and played a part in shaping the Pennsylvanian Constitution of 1776. But, almost inevitably, the war caused deep divisions not only between the lower-class 'patriots' and their allies but within popular radicalism itself. Unity continued, it appears, to fight monopoly and inflation during 1779; but, a year later, as mechanics became divided from poor artisans and labourers over the relative merits of *laissez-faire* and controls, a group of the militia representing the latter group marched into the city in the 'Fort Wilson' riot. This incident, added to the gradual conversion to *laissez-faire* of Thomas Paine, split the popular radical movement which, in the 1780s, ceased to make an impact either on the war or on the city's political life.[16]

So popular radicalism, whether in the form of crowd activity or of political organization, appears to have played a diminishing role once the war began. It may even be doubted whether, outside the larger towns and the northern rural areas, it played any part at all in drawing the common people into the 'patriot' cause. But, for lack of more certain knowledge, we may leave the answer to Alfred Young:

Given the inequalities of colonial society (which were very much worsened during the war), given the predemocratic character of the political scene and the premodern character of life for much of the country, it should not surprise us that many ordinary Americans had higher priorities than freedom from Britain. Blacks wanted their personal freedom; landless farmers wanted land; and women wanted the traditional concern of their 'sphere', the maintenance of hearth and home. Perhaps the wonder is that so many other Americans of humble circumstance saw their own aspirations bound up with independence. Historians still have to put the proportions in focus.[17]

NOTES

1. Historians have written of a black (Crispus Attucks) being killed in the Boston 'Massacre' and of many more who fought at Bunker Hill; but blacks were even more likely to side with the British than with the Americans, and their struggle for freedom from slavery would not come till more than fifty years later.

2. G. Nash, 'Social Change and the Growth of Prerevolutionary Urban Radicalism', in A. Young (ed.), *The American Revolution. Explorations in the History of American Radicalism* [henceforth cited as *Explorations*], DeKalb, 1976, p. 7.

3. ibid., pp. 8–9.

4. Edward Countryman, '"Out of the Bounds of the Law". Northern Land Rioters in the Eighteenth Century', in *Explorations*, pp. 37–69.

5. P. Maier, *From Resistance to Revolution*, New York, 1972, pp. 3–5.

6. Cit. Nash, p. 15.

7. ibid., pp. 18–27.

8. For the above, see mainly Dirk Hoerder, 'Boston Leaders and Boston Crowds, 1765–1766', in *Explorations*, pp. 235–62.

9. Eric Foner, 'Tom Paine's Republic: Radical Ideology and Social Change', in *Explorations*, pp. 194–6.

10. ibid., pp. 194–7.

11. B. Baylin, *The Ideological Origins of the American Revolution*, Harvard, 1967, p. 95; cit. Nash, p. 5.

12. J. Ernst, '"Ideology" and an Economic Interpretation of the Revolution,' in *Explorations*, pp. 161–82.

13. For the best study of the sailors' reaction to impressment at the end of the colonial period, see Jesse Lemisch, 'Jack Tar in the Street, Merchant Seamen in the Politics of Revolutionary America', *William & Mary Quarterly*, 25 (1968), 371–407.

14. Alfred Young's study, 'The Crowd in the Coming of the Revolution: from Ritual to Revolution in Boston', still awaits publication.

15. Nash, in *Explorations*, pp. 27–32.

16. Foner, pp. 197–220.

17. A. Young, in 'Afterword' to *Explorations*, p. 453.

3

The French Revolution

Of all revolutions, whether arising in industrial or 'preindustrial' times, none has been so well documented as the great French Revolution of the eighteenth century and in no other has the historian had access to such rich collections of papers relating to the lives, activities and manner of thinking of the common people. So the problem in this chapter will not be so much to scrape together such evidence as can be found, as to make a careful selection from the abundance available in order to keep it within reasonable limits.

As has been often observed, French society on the eve of the Revolution was more typical than any other of Europe of the Old Régime. Its principal features were: an absolute monarchy, still closely modelled on that created by Louis XIV over a century before; an aristocracy supported by privilege and wealth; a system of landholding that was still essentially feudal;[1] a merchant-bourgeoisie rivalling the English in wealth and status, but lacking all means of political control; a bureaucracy of venal office-holders that (and this was peculiarly French) had become so wealthy and independent that it threatened the security of the Throne that had created it; a vast peasantry accounting for one in seven or one in eight of the population, most of whom were legally free but bound to their *seigneur* (as we have seen before) by a myriad of services and obligations surviving from the medieval past. And, in cities, as also in Russia, Prussia, Italy, England and Spain, a great urban population of innumerable crafts and occupations, for the most part poor and depending for survival on cheap and plentiful bread.

All these social groups and classes were potentially revolutionary or committed to some form or other of political and social change. The aristocracy, divided between hereditary nobility and *noblesse de robe* (ennobled through purchase of office) but able to unite in moments of crisis, sought to redress in their favour the balance of power imposed on them by Louis XIV a century before, when he stripped them of all effective political control; in fact, the whole century was marked by their periodic attempts to do so. The bourgeoisie wanted a higher social status and a share in government commensurate with their wealth. The peasants wanted to rid themselves of all feudal burdens on the land and (most of them) to preserve their traditional village community; and the urban *menu peuple* (poorer classes) wanted a government that would assure them of a plentiful and regular supply of cheap food, particularly bread (their staple diet).

So it is not surprising that the successive economic crises of the 1770s and 1780s, which we referred to in an earlier chapter,[2] when compounded by a financial crisis following the American War, should have had such explosive results.

As is known, the aristocracy were the first to react in what has been called the 'révolte nobiliaire'; and this ended, as the result of combined aristocratic and popular pressure, in Louis XVI's historic decision to summon the Estates General to meet, for the first time for 175 years, at Versailles in May 1789. As is also well known, from this point the bourgeoisie, previously divided between those supporting the Parlements and aristocracy and those supporting the Royal government, united its forces and, with the aid of a popular insurrection in Paris, forced the aristocracy (now its main enemy) onto the defensive and formed a National Assembly, accepted by the King. As the result of this alliance between bourgeoisie and people, the Bastille was captured, an event that marked the real opening of the Revolution. Meanwhile, the peasants revolted in the summer of 1789 and, by burning the landlords' *châteaux* and manorial rolls, persuaded the National Assembly (composed of both bourgeois and clergy and liberal lords) to take note of their needs and take the first, decisive step, to dismantle the seigneurial system of land tenure.

But, of course, this could not have been done – nor could the subsequent events of the Revolution have taken place – without the existence of a revolutionary ideology to make it possible for the bourgeoisie – the new rulers – and the common people to make common cause to destroy the privileges of the aristocracy and the absolutism of the King. Where did this ideology come from? In the case of the bourgeoisie, the question is not a difficult one to answer. As the English revolutionaries of the seventeenth century had been inspired by the Bible and by the traditional assertion of its 'liberties' by Parliament against the King, so the French middle-class revolutionaries drew theirs from a purely secular source: the writings of the eighteenth-century *philosophes*, particularly those of Rousseau and Montesquieu through whose teaching they had learned to proclaim the principles of the Social Contract, the Rights of Man and Popular Sovereignty. And these, through all the changes and vicissitudes of revolution, remained the basic guide-lines of the revolutionary bourgeoisie.

The common people – the peasants and urban *menu peuple* – came to adopt a similar vocabulary and body of ideas, as is already evident from their slogans and actions in the months or weeks preceding the fall of the Bastille. But, basically, as we have seen in an earlier chapter, these classes came into the Revolution with 'inherent' and traditional ideas of their own: the peasants' demand for land and the integrity of their village community,[3] and the urban poor for a 'just price' to govern the distribution of bread. But how did they come to broaden their horizons and to develop, in addition, a wider political ideology, derived from that recently adopted by the new dominant revolutionary class, the bourgeoisie?

Historians concerned with this question (they are by no means in a majority) have approached it in a variety of ways; and we shall find that terms like *mentalité* and *sensibilité* (used by French writers and not easy to render in English) do not correspond exactly to what I mean by the 'inherent' element in ideology, and even less to what E. P. Thompson means by 'plebeian culture'.[4] Of French writers concerned with both 'culture' (in the French sense) and 'mentalité', Robert Mandrou has perhaps been the first in the field. In his *De la culture populaire aux 17e et 18e siècles*,[5] he uses the so-called 'blue' collection of books in the Library at Troyes, whose readers are presumed to have been predominantly lower-class, to discuss the degree to which the 'new' ideas, or any ideas, on history, science or politics were being absorbed by the *menu peuple*, to whom these books were addressed, by the middle of the eighteenth century. He finds no sign at all, not least because the authors had apparently been very careful to see that their books should contain no matter that might allow the common people who read them to stray, even in imagination, beyond the safe horizons of the aristocratic society in which they lived. So the picture of popular 'culture' that emerges is a thoroughly conformist and static one; in consequence, the study, while having a certain negative value, does not advance our enquiry by an inch.

Michel Vovelle raises different questions: what signs were there of a genuine pre-revolutionary 'sensibilité' (broadly, outlook or feelings) among the common people of France at any time before 1789? In a recent paper (published in English),[6] he brings forward ample evidence to show that, in the South at least, a change was taking place from about 1750 onwards in middle-class attitudes to death, burial, illegitimate births, marriage, God and religion and that some of this derived from the writings of the *philosophes*. He also found less certain evidence of a similarly changing attitude among craftsmen and tradesmen to funeral practices, in particular, but very little else and most certainly no sign of the percolation among such groups of the 'new' or 'philosophical' writings of the Enlightenment. But he also points to other sources of popular culture, such as the charivari, the carnival and the *confrérie* (with its religious associations). The primitive and often brutal ideology revealed in these can, he believes, be followed through to the riots of the early revolutionary years, including the notorious September Massacres of 1792.

As my own concern is to show how the 'derived' element in popular ideology became superimposed on, and absorbed by, the 'inherent' element that already existed, my treatment will, of course, be different from those I have cited above. I have thought it best to attempt to trace the emergence of a popular *prise de conscience* and revolutionary ideology by considering in turn the different modes of popular activity and the thought that accompanied them during the last fifteen years of the Old Régime. To start with the corn riots (the 'guerre des farines') of which mention has been made in an earlier chapter.[7] These were the riots that convulsed half a dozen provinces (involving both Paris and Versailles) lying within a 100 to 150-mile radius of the capital. At first sight, as the rioters were mainly villagers, it looks like a large-scale peasant movement anticipating the great peasant rebellion of 1789. Yet, on closer inquiry, it turns out to have been not a strictly *peasant* movement at all, but one of small consumers not so different, except for its scope, from many others of its kind that broke out intermittently in periods of shortage between the 1720s and 1780s. In them there was no intrusion at all of the 'new' ideas (Rousseau's *Emile* and *Social Contract* had first been published a dozen years before) nor was there any attempt to settle accounts with the *seigneurs* or clergy (unless they happened, like other proprietors, to be hoarding or storing grain); and indeed, in spite of earlier explanations to the contrary, there was no sign either of any political 'intrusion', even by Turgot's enemies at Court.[8] And, as I have said, similar movements with their familiar form of imposing a 'just' price on grain continued, on a more muted scale, up to the Revolution – and, in fact, far beyond it.

For wage-earners, the alternative method of social protest was the strike; and there were several confrontations of this kind – particularly among paper, printing and building workers and porters – in the last fifteen years before the Revolution began. A French labour historian, Marcel Rouff, who wrote about these movements over half a century ago, thought that the strike of the porters, who (in 1786) marched to the Royal Palace at Versailles to present their demands, was of particular interest and wrote of it as if it were almost a prelude to revolution.[9] This is, however, to take a rather over-optimistic view, as strikes (as noted by Daniel Mornet a couple of decades later) were still comparatively unimportant and certainly far less frequent and less significant than food riots. For this was still the age of the small workshop, when the typical master craftsman worked in close proximity to his half-dozen journeymen and apprentices. Such wage-earners shared, at second hand, the views of their masters except at occasional moments of dispute over wages; so it is not surprising that we should not look there for any signs of a popular political awakening until the masters themselves were ready to receive and to convey the message.[10]

So we must look elsewhere – to the food riot which, although a-political in 1775 as we have seen, began to be 'politicized' in the early autumn of 1788 towards the end of the 'aristocratic revolt'. The occasion was the news of the return of the Parlement to Paris after its second exile and the popular excitement this aroused in a period of steeply rising prices. It was the concordance of the two that brought the working people of the Faubourgs into the streets; and Hardy, the bookseller-diarist, whose shop off the Boulevard St Germain in the University quarter provided him with an excellent vantage point for observing what went on in the streets, noted in early September that troops had been brought in to overawe the common people, 'dont le [Gouvernement] avait à craindre l'Insurrection'; and, as prices continued to rise, he noted a significant development: that working housewives were beginning (from November onwards) to direct their complaints and imprecations from the bakers to the Government and Royal princes, and even to the King himself.[11] This was the beginning of a popular political understanding, the dawn of a *crise de conscience*, reaching far beyond the earlier mouthing of slogans in support of the Parlement; because the issue – the issue of bread – touched them more closely. But it was not yet the beginning of a *revolutionary* ideology; this was still to come.

It might perhaps have been expected to appear first at Lyons, where the common people – or the silk-weavers of the great 'Fabrique', at least – had a far longer and more continuous tradition of militancy than craftsmen in Paris. The eighteenth century had seen a series of violent conflicts between the weavers, led by their *maîtres-ouvriers* (who themselves employed labour) and the *marchands-fabricants*, who controlled the industry. In the last great confrontation – that of 1786 – the weavers had fought for the Tarif (or minimum wage) and had for the first time seen themselves as a class exploited by their masters. The hostility engendered between the two was such that when the 'Fabrique' was later called upon to meet and appoint delegates to draw up a *cahier de doléances* for the local Third Estate to take along to Versailles, the *maîtres-ouvriers* (representing the silk workers) succeeeded in squeezing out the merchants and in filling all the seats themselves. So an opportunity was offered for the workers' voice to be heard not only at Lyons but at Versailles as well. But, astonishing as it must seem, the challenge was never taken up. The worker-delegates merely drew up a *cahier* intended to favour the 'Fabrique' as a whole; no reference was made to the particular needs of the workers, or even of the needs of the people at large; and they dutifully sent forward educated people like merchants and lawyers to represent them at Versailles.[12] And they continued to fail to rise to the occasion and to play second fiddle to their employers, even during the period of counter-revolution in the summer of 1793.

Why should this have happened? The only answer that makes much sense is that the Lyonnais workers were organized within a vast Corporation ('Fabrique'), which also included their employers; and, in spite of their militancy and class-awareness, they lacked the intimacy of the small workshop in Paris which brought masters and journeymen into easy association and acted as one of the two principal conveyor-belts for the transmission of (bourgeois) revolutionary ideas. (The other, as has already been suggested, was the market or baker's shop.) And this, in contrast to Lyons, was the situation in Paris where most industry was carried on in these small workshops with their strong medieval flavour. But first – before there were revolutionary ideas to transmit – the opportunity had to be offered by the Royal summons for the Estates to meet at Versailles. The result (as Georges Lefebvre reminds us) was electric.[13] On the one hand, it roused the 'great hope' of a national regeneration, which, as witnessed by Arthur Young on his travels through the French countryside, roused the peasants as well as the people of the towns.[14] Secondly, it provoked a great stream of literature in the form of published *cahiers*, pamphlets and petitions in preparation for the great assembly at Versailles. Among them was one document that was to prove of capital importance: the Abbé Sieyès' pamphlet *'Qu'est-ce que le tiers état? (What is the Third Estate?)*, which for the first time declared that the Third Estate (or bourgeoisie), representing the nation as a whole, was ready to take over the government of the country, whether the nobility decided to join it or not. The term 'third estate', repeated in markets, at street corners and in innumerable workshops, soon entered into popular speech; I have found its use by a Paris craftsman recorded in a police report of 21 April.[15] A week later, it was one of the slogans shouted in the Réveillon riots in the Faubourg St Antoine; the others were 'Vive le Roi!' and 'Vive M. Necker!' (both were popular heroes of the hour). Soon after, it became extended into the more militant challenge, 'es-tu du tiers état?', which (so he records) greeted the future *sans-culotte* general, Jean Rossignol, when he arrived in Paris that summer to take up his craft as a journeyman goldsmith;[16] and Arthur Young had to respond to it affirmatively – to save his skin, as he believed – on a country road a few weeks later. By this time, it appears that, in the mouth of the people, the term 'tiers état' – soon to be followed by others such as 'contrat social' and 'droits de l'homme' – had undergone a transformation. To them it no longer denoted the 'nation' or the 'bourgeoisie' (and Sieyès was as likely to mean the one as the other), but themselves, the common people, or at least such of them as took up the cudgels against 'aristocracy'. How else explain the choice of the slogan 'vive le tiers état' by those destroying Réveillon's house in April? For Réveillon and his fellow-victim Henriot, both manufacturers of the Faubourg, were elected representatives for their districts to the Third Estate in Paris. A further adaptation in common speech followed soon after. As the political crisis at Versailles deepened with the sustained refusal of the 'privileged orders' to join the Third Estate in forming a National Assembly, every opponent of the 'tiers' became an enemy of the Nation and, whether nobleman or not, an 'aristocrat' as well. And as, in response to both political and economic crises, more and more of the *menu peuple* – labourers as well as craftsmen – were being swept along by the revolutionary current, these first lessons and vocabulary of revolution were being absorbed by ever wider circles. On the eve of the capture of the Bastille, Jean-Nicholas Pepin, a tallow-chandler's porter, arrested among the swirling crowds that filled the city's streets, explained his behaviour in terms that had by now become familiar:

> . . . we were bringing help to the Nation against the enemies that wanted to destroy all Parisians; and [he added] the enemies were the *noblesse*.[17]

It would, however, be fair to say that the events taking place at Versailles – compounded, of course, by the economic crisis – had a more profound effect on the villages than they had on the towns. It was not so much that the new ideas of the Revolution roused the peasants (as we have already suggested, notions like 'le tiers etat' arrived in the village considerably later than in the city) as that the old traditional, 'inherent' idea, based on the age-old hostility of the rural population to feudal dues and taxes, which had lain dormant during a large part of the eighteenth century, rose to the surface and fused the peasants, divided as they had been between landed and landless and rich and poor proprietors, into a single class that, with remarkably little aid from the towns, was able to carry through what Lefebvre has called a 'peasant revolution' in July–August 1789. But, as we have noted elsewhere, the peasants were not satisfied by the half-baked settlement of the land question enacted in the days that followed; in consequence, the peasant rebellion, though it never reached the heights of the summer of 1789, simmered on with occasional violent outbreaks until the final settlement – 'final', that is, as far as the 'middling' and wealthier peasants were concerned – was made by the Jacobins in June–July 1793. (The events of the Vendée were, of course, a different matter; I shall return to them briefly later.)

But it is probably only in Paris (and not in Lyons or Rouen or Bordeaux among the cities) that sufficient exploratory work has been done by historians to make it possible to present a reasonably faithful picture of the subsequent evolution of popular ideology. This development depended partly on the means provided by the bourgeois democrats and others in terms of newspapers, open-air meetings, popular societies (beginning in 1791), the galleries of the National Assembly and Jacobin Club – and partly on the people's direct experience as they participated more fully in revolution. The next important stage in this process after October 1789 was marked by the dramatic events of the summer of 1791: Louis' attempted flight and forced return to Paris; his provisional suspension and subsequent reinstatement in office, leading to the emergence of a powerful democratic and radical opposition to the liberal-monarchist majority, in which a leading part was played by the Jacobins' rival, the more plebeian Cordeliers Club.[18] The agitation led to a further radicalization of the craftsmen and labourers of Paris (by now being called '*sans-culottes*' by their more genteel opponents), who began to attend the meetings of the Sections and enrol in the National Guard (from both of which they were still officially excluded) and flocked into the Champ de Mars in July 1791 to sign or set their mark on a petition calling for the King's abdication and were violently dispersed by sabres and bullets. By this time, they were attending meetings of popular societies, demanding the right to vote, and even reading the radical press.[19] This all served to educate the *sans-culottes* further in the vocabulary and ideas of the revolutionary bourgeoisie – journalists, orators and politicians – who, based on both Jacobin and Cordeliers Clubs, were giving the Revolution a decisive turn to the left.

The next important stage in the development of popular ideology came with the Jacobin victory over their Girondin rivals in the National Convention, and the emergence of a Jacobin majority, strongly supported by the *sans-culottes* to whose demands they were compelled to pay attention (as in the Laws of the Maximum, placing a ceiling on prices, in September 1793). Meanwhile, encouraged by the Jacobins, the *sans-culottes* were taking over the sixty Sections, most of which they dominated by August, and gradually filling the majority of councillors' seats in the city's Commune as well. So, by the time the Jacobins formed their 'revolutionary government' at the end of the year, the *sans-culottes* not only held the leading posts of command in the capital but were also developing a life-style and policies of their own distinctive from, and generally at variance with, those of their Jacobin teachers.[20] Their ideas on property were those of all small producers and shopkeepers, typical of those who spoke and voted in the Sections: they opposed its unrestricted use by wealthier citizens who claimed the right to do what they liked with it. But they had no intention to support an 'agrarian law' or to divide up property into equal proportions; the farthest they were willing to go was to demand a limitation in the size of properties and property rights in the interests of a community of small producers like themselves. Such a demand was voiced most coherently and explicitly by the Section des Sans-Culottes on 2 September 1793, when they insisted, among other things, that 'no one should own more than one workshop, or one store'.[21] They also demanded progressive taxation in the interests of the poor, and equality of social benefits (*égalité des jouissances*), including free education and cheap bread; and they objected to the merger of small workshops into larger units for wartime production. Their political demands posed greater problems for the Jacobin Government for they demanded 'direct democracy', or the right to meet 'permanently' in their Sections and popular societies, to recall deputies at will, to parade armed before the Assembly when the spirit moved them, and even to call out the Sections in rebellion ('l'insurrection est le plus sacré des devoirs') should the Government fail in its duties to the people.

In consequence, as Soboul has amply shown, relations between *sans-culottes* and Jacobins became progressively more strained; their hostility (of the wage-earners, in particular, when threatened with a massive cut in wages) helped to bring the Jacobins down; and ironically, Jacobins and *sans-culottes* went down together, the victims of a conspiracy hatched by opponents on both right and left but from which the right alone gained all the rewards.

So the *sans-culottes*, like the Jacobins, were silenced and, for many months, they nursed their grievances and waited for a better day. It never came; but, strangely enough, the height of *sans-culotte* independence – of action and thought – came in their two final uprisings of Germinal and Prairial of the Year III (March and May 1795), when they invaded the Assembly, demanding bread, the release of the imprisoned 'patriots' (Jacobins and 'Hébertists'), and the restoration of the Paris Commune (reduced to impotence by the 'Thermidorians') and of the democratic Constitution of June 1793 (put into cold storage 'for the duration' by the Jacobins but scrapped altogether by their successors); and they compelled the reluctant Jacobin remnants in the Assembly to voice their demands. The episode ended in defeat and led to nothing more than the further persecution of both Jacobins and *sans-culottes* who now, through terror, were more effectively, and more permanently, silenced than they had been before. But it had its importance as marking the high-point of independent popular ideology during the Revolution (if we except the communist-egalitarian ideas of Babeuf which found no popular audience at the time). For here, for the first time in the Revolution, the *sans-culottes* organized a political *journée* of their own, marched to overthrow the Assembly with their own slogans, banners and leaders, and voiced their own demands, infused by their own ideology.[22]

The memory of these 'days', and of the others before them, survived and we shall see that memory brought to life in subsequent revolutions and 'événements' in France's later history. Materially, the *sans-culottes* had gained very little from the Revolution: the right to vote and the controls on food prices had been withdrawn before the end of 1795. But, most certainly, they had left their mark on events. First, they had served as the shock-troops of revolution in all the great public events that successively overthrew the Bastille, fetched the King and Queen back to Paris in October, brought down the monarchy, removed the Girondins from the Assembly and brought the Jacobins to power, compelled the Jacobin-dominated Convention to enact the Maximum laws and other social measures. Secondly, although never holding more than a handful of seats in the National Assemblies of the Revolution, it was the first time that small craftsmen and tradesmen had ruled a city the size of Paris for a whole critical year. And, thirdly (and this is almost to repeat what we have said before), despite the loss of their more 'material' gains, the tradition of mass popular action and 'direct' democracy, initiated by the Paris *sans-culottes*, and many of the ideas that went with them, survived. We shall hear more of them in our next chapter.

ADDENDUM

Paris was, of course, not typical of France although the euphoria of the summer of 1789, allowing for the necessary time-lag, was probably universal. There was a certain parting of the ways among peasants already by the end of 1791 (particularly in parts of Brittany, where the imposition of new priests after the Constitution of the Clergy and its condemnation by the Pope caused great dissatisfaction); but it became more widespread later.

The great year of dissent was 1793, when not only the Vendée – followed by the peasant guerrillas (*chouans*) of Lower Brittany and NW Normandy – but also half a dozen of France's largest cities – were in open revolt. The breaking-point in the Vendée came with the *levée en masse*, which was believed both to be unfairly administered by bureaucrats taking their orders from faraway Paris and (reasonably enough) to threaten to leave the fields denuded of labour for the coming harvest. So the Breton peasants, while no less anxious to complete the 'revolution' in the village than those in the rest of France, were thrown into the arms of the most reactionary nobility of the Old Régime, amply supported by 'Pitt's gold' (not illusory this time!).

The 'federal revolt', mainly centred on Lyons, Marseille and Bordeaux, was largely promoted by the wealthy merchant-class, whose politics since the Revolution began had always been moderate and whose Jacobin Clubs, except briefly at Lyons, had been of the 'Girondin' rather than the 'Jacobin' type. The expulsion of the Girondin deputies from the Convention and their subsequent persecution were the signal for revolts that, inevitably, attracted royalist support. The master craftsmen in these cities appear to have been drawn into the 'federalist' camp; and the journeymen, though often hostile to the merchants, appear to have been too much weakened by division to attempt to intervene and were carried along with the tide. (For a brief study of these divisions and the line-up of parties at Bordeaux, see Alan Forrest, *Society and Politics in Revolutionary Bordeaux*, Oxford, 1975, esp. pp. 159–80.)

For the blending of 'inherent' and 'derived' elements of popular ideology in such situations, the reader is referred back to the argument presented on p. 35 above.

NOTES

1. The use of the term 'feudal' here is obviously contentious; but the author has not been sufficiently impressed by the recent arguments put forward by a (mainly) British and American group of 'revisionist' historians to abandon it.

2. See pp. 64–5 above, and Labrousse's Introduction to his *Crise de l'économie française*, pp. ix–xli.

3. For a recent study of peasant outlook and demands on the eve of the Revolution, see Florence Gauthier, *La voie paysanne dans la Révolution française; l'exemple de la Picardie*, Paris, 1977.

4. See p. 31 above.

5. Paris, 1964; reprint in 1978.

6. M. Vouvelle, 'Le tournant des mentalités en France 1750–1789: la sensibilité pré-révolutionnaire' (in English translation) in *Social History*, 5, May 1977, pp. 605–29.

7. See pp. 64–5 above.

8. For the most complete treatment summing up all the evidence, see Edgar Faure, *La Disgrâce de Turgot*, Paris, 1961.

9. M. Rouff, 'Une grève de gagne-deniers en 1786 à Paris', *Revue hist.*, CLXV (1910), 332–46.

10. G. Rudé, *The Crowd in the French Revolution*, Oxford 1959, pp. 21–2, 134, 146.

11. S. Hardy, 'Mes loisirs, ou journal d'événements tels qu'ils parviennent à ma connoissance' (MS. in 8 vols, 1764–89, Bib. Nationale, fonds français, nos. 6680–7), VIII, 73, 154–5, 250: entries for 5 September, 25 November 1788, 13 February 1789.

12. See M. Garden, *Lyon et les lyonnais au XVIIIe siècle*, Paris, 1970, esp. pp. 552–92; J. Jaurès, *Histoire socialiste de la Révolution française*, A. Soboul (ed.), 7 vols, 1968–73, Paris, I, 177–8.

13. G. Lefebvre, *Quatre-Vingt-Neuf*, Paris, 1939, p. 112.

14. A. Young, *Travels in France during the years 1787–1788–1789* . . . New York, 1969, p. 144.

15. Arch. Nat., Y 18762.

16. A. Mathiez, *Les grandes journées de la Constituante*, Paris, 1913, pp. 23–5.

17. Arch. Nat., Z^2 4691 (my translation).

18. The best account of this process is still that given by Mathiez in *Le Club des Cordeliers pendant la crise de Varennes et le massacre de Champ du Mars*, Paris, 1910.

19. See the police interrogation of Constance Evrard, a 23-year-old cook, arrested after the Champ de Mars Affray: in my *Crowd*, pp. 86–7.

20. For this and much of what follows, see Albert Soboul, *The Parisian Sans-Culottes and the French Revolution 1793–4*, Oxford, 1964.

21. ibid., p. 64.

22. For this episode and its antecedents, see K. Thönesson, *La défaite des sans-culottes*, Oslo, 1959.

4

French Revolutions of the Nineteenth Century

The French revolutions of the nineteenth century, though arising in response to quite particular problems and situations, had much in common and may, therefore, be treated within a single chapter. Unlike the three earlier revolutions considered, they occurred in a society which, though subject to gradual change, had already had its main features determined by the revolution of 1789, and by the industrial revolution that began, somewhat hesitantly, about the end of the 1820s. Through the first revolution the aristocratic society of the Old Régime, while recovering a certain ground under the Restoration monarchs who followed Napoleon, had become essentially *bourgeois* and only awaited the impact of an industrial revolution to set it firmly on a course that would lead it into the industrial and capitalist society of the 1880s.

As elsewhere, the main features of such a society were the emergence of a manufacturing employing class and a class of industrial workers, or proletarians, and a gradual tendency to become polarized between the two. But, unlike Britain, the process was a slow one, largely due to the long survival of intermediate traditional classes (as noted by Gramsci in Italy) of small shopkeepers, self-employed petty producers and, above all, a large peasantry to which the great Revolution had given a degree of stability that, throughout the nineteenth century, defied the inroads of capitalist industrialization. Eventually France, too, would embark on rapid capitalist expansion, but this remained for the future and in the largely 'pre-industrial' society with which we shall be concerned in the present chapter, change was comparatively slow and its pattern uneven. It is true that there were 5,000 steam engines in operation in France in 1847 where there had been only 2,000 in operation seven years before (but this compared with ten times that number in Britain). Again, France's railway network of 2,000 miles in 1850 compared with 5,000 miles in England, and even Germany had 3,000. City populations had admittedly grown, but only in a few

– such as Lille, Roubaix or St Etienne – as the result of industrialization. Paris, the great city of revolutions – even more in the nineteenth than in the eighteenth century – had a population of about 550,000 in 1800, which had doubled by 1850 and reached 1¾ million by 1870. But though industrial districts – centres of railway workshops, cotton and light engineering – were sprouting from the 1840s on, Paris remained largely a city of small workshops, manufactories, homeworkers and petty crafts; and even at the time of the Commune in 1871, only about one in ten of its industrial workers worked in large-scale industry or in undertakings employing a hundred people or more.[1]

But this was not the whole story: though social and industrial change was slow, the great division marking the new industrial society was already under way and by the late 1820s, at least, the single-class *ouvrier* had already replaced the petty-bourgeois oriented *sans-culotte* as the main protagonist of social protest and the wage-earners, even those working as *compagnons* in small workshops, were no longer so closely tied to the apron-strings of their masters. And, equally significant, due no doubt to the pervasive influence of the French Revolution, the *ouvrier* would, by the 1840s, allowing imagination to enrich experience, assume the title of *prolétaire* (first used in its more-or-less modern sense by Blanqui in 1832) at a time when the British worker, though *objectively* better qualified, was not yet subjectively prepared to do so. But this, of course, was also a gradual process and one that we shall attempt to follow through the successive revolutions of 1830, 1848 and 1871.

In July 1830 Charles X, the second of the Restoration monarchs, was toppled from his throne by an alliance of liberal (though wealthy) bourgeois, to whom Charles had denied the freedoms enshrined in the Charter of 1814, and the *ouvriers* of the various crafts of Paris. After three days' fighting – 'les Trois Glorieuses' – the Orleanist Pretender, Louis Philippe, was hustled on to the throne by a combination of bankers and journalists and acclaimed by the people at the City Hall. This is the short account of the revolution as traditionally narrated. But, of course, there was much more to it than that, as modern historians, several of them American, have shown. In the first place, the outcome was not to everybody's satisfaction: of the two partners, 'la blouse et la redingote', as Edgar Newman has called them,[2] the 'blouse' (the workers) was cheated and the victory was exploited in the sole interest of the 'redingote' (the employers). But the workers refused to play the part of pulling the chestnuts out of the fire for the bourgeoisie and, having played their part, began to put forward claims of their own. It was the printing workers, whose jobs depended on the continued survival of the Paris newspapers, that set the example: they were just as alarmed by Charles's anti-liberal Ordinances of St Cloud as the bourgeois journalists and politicians. So it was they that first came on to the streets and gave a lead to the other Paris crafts which David Pinkney has shown to have provided (like their forebears in July 1789) the bulk of the protesters. Their motives were two-fold: to protect their own jobs and liberties and to express their patriotic resentment, alongside their bourgeois allies, against the despotic actions of the Bourbon King.[3] But there were other motives as well: the revolution broke out in the wake of a deep economic crisis that caused a sharp rise in the price of food; and many had their own ideas about what government should follow. It was not, as often claimed, the Republic; but, according to Newman's study of what the crowd actually wanted in 1830, a return to Napoleon.[4]

But, among these factors, there were also, as usual, other forms of return to the past as well: old-style food riots exploded, as in 1775, in response to the high price of bread; peasants in the Ariège, disguised as 'demoiselles', drove out the forest guards to defend their traditional rights of pasture;[5] in the name of 'liberty' workers destroyed machines that deprived them of the right to work; and, also in the name of 'liberty' but far more significant of changing times, they demanded the right to organize in workers' associations, or trade unions, to defend their wages and conditions of work.

So the revolution of 1830, as far as the liberal bourgeoisie was concerned, had completed the 'unfinished business' of the first revolution by giving a safe constitutional home to the 'principles of 1789'; yet, in the process, the settlement created 'unfinished business' of another kind as the experiences of the next few years would show. For the *ouvriers*, the struggle they embarked on in 1830 had been only a beginning. The first workers' newspapers, the *Journal des Ouvriers* and others, began to appear in 1831, and they would devote many columns to the crying need for association. Other developments of the 1830s and 1840s are also of prime importance; so that before we go on to the revolution of 1848 we must consider the series of workers' insurrections that broke out first at Lyons and later in Paris, and the ideological developments that accompanied them. For, in the course of these battles, the French working-class – fighting on both economic and political fronts – was born.

It was at Lyons, as we saw in the last chapter, that, as a result of the bitter conflicts waged within the silk industry between the *canuts* (master and journeyman silk-weavers) and the merchant-manufacturers, a rudimentary consciousness of class had first appeared on the eve of the revolution of 1789. The silk industry, like the city of Lyons itself, had been deeply scarred by the Revolution; and there, as elsewhere in France, the Le Chapelier Law of 1791 had forbidden workers to combine. The silk industry (accounting for half the city's trade and a quarter of its income) had recovered by 1830 and was undergoing a period of great prosperity. But the *canuts*' dissatisfaction (far from being appeased) had been increased by the spread of the industry into the countryside, the new *laissez-faire* methods that denied them the paternalist protection of the old 'Fabrique', and by the introduction during the early years of the century of the labour-saving Jacquard loom. Moreover, to give that dissatisfaction more effective expression, far earlier than in other parts of France, the silk-weavers within the city limits lived and worked in densely inhabited suburbs like La Croux Rousse and Parrache that already constituted identifiable working-class districts.[6]

Though a common euphoria briefly united *canuts* and merchants after the fall of Charles X in Paris, the spell was soon broken by the merchants' refusal to pay serious attention to the *canuts*' renewed demand for a *tarif* (scale of wages and prices). So, in November 1831, the weavers who, following the July events, had easy access to arms, rose in rebellion, chanting their famous slogan *Vivre en travaillant ou mourir en combattant* ('live working or die fighting'), overpowered the local garrison with unexpected ease, and found themselves in control of the city. A newspaper warned, 'The barbarians who menace society are neither in the Caucasus nor on the Tartar steppes; they are in the suburbs of our manufacturing cities.'[7] But the workers lacked organization and political understanding and did not know what to do with their victory. So they accepted a compromise and returned to their districts.

The next round came soon enough. The journeymen weavers, having discovered the need for organization, followed their masters' example by enrolling in the Society of Mutual Duty, which, by December 1833, had become a less exclusive and more militant body, and prepared for a general strike. Meanwhile, two things happened: the Paris Government intervened and banned Mutuellism together with other workers' associations and began to arrest its members; and the local Republican party (with its offshoot, the Society of the Rights of Man), up to now cold-shouldered by the weavers' community, took up the Mutuellists' cause, demonstrated against the new law on associations, and gave significant support to the weavers' second uprising when it broke out in April 1834. The uprising – the largest civil disturbance in France between 1830 and 1848 – lasted six days and left over 300 dead. But this time the local authorities and garrison were prepared, and the weavers and their Republican allies were beaten into submission, leaving 500 prisoners in the hands of justice. Yet the event was of great historical importance as it marked the entry of the largest body of industrial workers in France into political association – however tenuous at first – with the Republican movement. But (as Robert Bezucha insists) the real political education of the Lyonnais workers, outraged by the Government's exploitation of its victory, followed rather than accompanied their uprising.[8]

Meanwhile, the first of the Lyons insurrections had provoked a series of workers' protests and rebellions in other cities in France – all the more readily as delegates from Paris, Marseille and other cities had come to Lyons to learn from its example. The first of the Paris outbreaks, and the most violent, occurred on 5–6 June 1832, following the funeral of a popular Bonapartist general, in the cloisters of St Méri, in the crowded central market area; 70 troops and 80 rioters were killed and of a couple of hundred prisoners taken, a large number were craftsmen – both masters and journeymen. Of these several will reappear in later riots: one, a journeyman baker, who was arrested for taking part in a wages dispute a few weeks later. (The point, though it may seem trivial, is important as it illustrates that, by this time, the same workers were engaging successively in political and industrial movements – in itself an important innovation.)[9] The second Paris outbreak occurred in April 1834, a few days after news arrived in the city of the April events at Lyons; it followed the closure of the radical-Republican *Tribune* and the arrest of the leaders of the Paris section of the Society of the Rights of Man. Troops shot down demonstrating workers in the Marais and Temple districts, lying to the north of the City Hall. The outbreak was on a far smaller scale than the first; but it became immortalized by Daumier's cartoon, 'The Massacre of the Rue Transnonain'. The third outbreak came four years later and had more precise political objectives than the others; it took the form of an armed attempt to overthrow the Government by Auguste Blanqui and his Society of the Four Seasons in 1839.

This was the last of the workers' political rebellions of the 1830s and a lull now followed until 1848. But, meanwhile, other developments of equal significance were taking shape. One was the emergence of Republican societies with a radical-democratic programme that not only gave political education to the workers but enrolled them in large numbers as members. The largest and most important of these was the Society of the Rights of Man which, already in 1834, had about 3,000 members, four in every five of whom were industrial workers.[10] Another development was the emergence between the 1820s and 1840s of a number of writers – a new breed of *philosophes* – who, though trained in the middle-class democratic principles of the revolution of 1789, often gave a new 'socialist' content to the Jacobin notion of the Rights of Man and directed their pamphlets and books as much to working-class as to middle-class readers. The most influential of these works were St Simon's and Fourier's blueprints for a planned industrial society; Etienne Cabet's primitive-communist dream of an Icarian Utopia; Pierre Leroux's writings on socialism (he invented the term); Buonarroti's *Conspiracy of the Equals* based on Babeuf's ill-starred 'conspiracy' of 1796; Louis Blanc's *Organization of Labour*, the model for the 'social' workshops intended in 1848; and Proudhon's *What is Property?*, a founding manifesto of anarchism. And some of these writers (Louis Blanc, for example) clearly drew their inspiration from the working-class movement at Lyon, as Marx would later learn lessons from the factory workers' movement in England to help in the writing of *Capital*.[11]

So, armed with ideas such as these – a medley of utopian-socialist systems and more practical solutions to meet immediate needs – the Parisians were able to enter the revolution of 1848 with an ideology, largely derived from professional writers of the middle class, but which the cadres at least – the leaders and members of the democratic clubs – had already digested before the revolution began and in the process had given the old Jacobins' democratic principles a twist of their own. Alexis de Tocqueville, an astute observer, sensed the new spirit and warned the Chamber of Deputies a month before the outbreak that the 'working classes' are gradually forming opinions and ideas which are destined not only to upset this or that law, ministry, or even form of government, but society itself'.[12]

The revolution that followed took place in two main stages: in February and in June 1848. In February, as in July 1830, the Paris workers and bourgeoisie (though this time it was the 'middling' and professional bourgeoisie) joined forces to overthrow the government of Louis Philippe; but, this time, too, the alliance, though shortlived, gave the workers some temporary advantages by forming a Provisional Government, on which the socialists were represented, and quickly carried through a number of agreed measures, such as male adult suffrage, a moratorium on debts and the declaration of the Second Republic. Even before the alliance fell apart a few weeks later, Marx, who had few illusions, termed the outcome the creation of a 'bourgeois republic', though one 'surrounded by social institutions'. Tocqueville probably had no illusions either; but, as a champion of property, he saw such dangers as there were and declared that the February event 'had been made entirely outside the bourgeoisie and against it'; and he added (almost as if he anticipated Marx's 'spectre that is haunting Europe') that 'socialism will always remain the essential characteristic and most redoubtable remembrance of the Revolution of February'.[13]

Property-owners generally must have shared Tocqueville's

feelings when, after the April elections, he 'saw society cut into two: those who possessed nothing united in a common greed; those who possessed something in a common terror'. So there was bound to be a show-down between the two, a battle in the streets, and the sooner it came the better.[14] Marx agreed with Tocqueville that, from the bourgeois point of view, 'a second battle was necessary in order to sever the republic from the socialist concessions' and that 'the bourgeoisie had to refute the demands of the proletariat with arms in its hands'.[15] When it came. in June, as Tocqueville both anticipated and hoped, the two men, though diametrically opposed to each other's political views, were agreed as to its nature. To Tocqueville it was 'a struggle of class against class, a sort of Servile War'; and to Marx 'the first great battle . . . between the two classes that split modern society'. To both its outcome – the inevitable defeat of the workers who had had the battle thrust upon them – established the bourgeois Republic on firmer foundations; yet Marx looked further ahead and argued that from now on revolution (and not only in France) meant 'overthrow of bourgeois society, whereas, before February, it had meant overthrow of the form of state'.[16]

Yet, even if the June 'days' were indeed the historical dividing-line of which Marx wrote, it would be absurd to imagine that even the most politically articulate of the workers who fought on the barricades were aware of it. These were still in their majority the craftsmen of the traditional trades of Paris. There had, it is true, been changes since 1789 and 1830. With the advent of railways, for one thing, railway repair shops and marshalling yards and other related trades had sprung up to the north of the city; and there were railwaymen and mechanics, and also considerable numbers of building workers, that fought on the barricades alongside the small masters and journeymen of the traditional crafts and appear with them on the long lists of those condemned to prison or transportation after the defeat. So there was an important change in the composition of the rioters from that in earlier revolutions, but this was not so marked as the change in their ideology. Their slogans in June did not call for the overthrow of capitalism (this was not yet an issue) but, following the lessons learned in the 1830s, for 'the Organization of labour by association' and for that 'Democratic and Social Republic' all hopes of which appeared to be shattered by the June defeat and which were dealt an even more shattering blow by the advent to power of Louis Napoleon, first as President and later as Emperor. But that there were those who, even in defeat, nourished such hopes is proved by the survival of a note dictated to the police from La Roquette prison by Antoine Bisgamblia, an obscure and illiterate mechanic, who had been arrested in June. In it he expressed his convictions – and hopes for the future – as follows:

> Everybody knows that I don't compromise my conscience and that, as long as I have breath left in my body, I shall use it for the triumph of the Democratic and Social Republic.[17]

But, paradoxically, after the Paris workers' defeat and the decimation of their cadres by firing-squad, prison and transportation, it was the peasants – mainly the peasants and village artisans of the South – who took up the cudgels for the Democratic Republic both through the votes they cast for Ledru-Rollin and his socio-democratic party in the elections of 1849 and (less widely) in armed rebellion against the first of Louis Napoleon's *coups d'état* in December 1851. I say 'paradoxically' because of the peasants' earlier role and the negative reputation historians have given them for their virtual abstention (except in old-style food riots) in February, their intervention against the Paris workers in June, and their massive vote in support of Louis Napoleon as President in December 1848 (Marx called it ironically the '*real* peasant revolution'). This was understandable in view of the peasants' deep resentment at the Provisional Government's enactment of the 'forty-five centimes tax' levied to finance its social benefits, which appeared as a subsidy to Paris at the peasants' expense. Besides, at this stage, there were few signs of peasant sympathy for the workers' democratic and 'socialist' ideas, or even for the bourgeois-democratic solutions offered by Lamartine or Ledru-Rollin. Yet peasant conservative attitudes, begotten by the substantial gains won in the first revolution, were already changing and, in some regions of the South, had been doing so steadily from 1830 on. Maurice Agulhon, whose studies of peasant culture and politics over these years have opened entirely new perspectives, relates an 1832 report expressing official alarm at the indoctrination of the craftsmen of Draguignan, the semi-rural capital of the Var, with liberal-democratic ideas passed on to them in wine-shops and cafés by 'half-baked intellectuals' and *déclassé* elements (the phrases have a familiar ring!).[18] And he goes on to describe how the peasants' traditional culture of folklore, far from acting as a conservative barrier to radicalization, merged with it and produced (to quote Agulhon again) 'the integration of new political acquisitions with spontaneous syncretic folklore'.[19] These 'acquisitions' had, by 1849, come to include widespread village support for Ledru-Rollin's *démocrate-socialiste* party in the Massif Central, the Saône and Rhône valleys, and coastal regions of the South;[20] and, two years later, when Louis Napoleon staged the first of his *coups d'état* in Paris, 25–30,000 peasants of the southern Alpine and coastal departments sprang to arms 'not [in Peter Amann's words] in support of an alien constitution, but on behalf of a revolutionary republic in the making'.[21] M. Agulhon adds that, in the Var, most militant of the Mediterranean departments, it was the organized peasants, many of them working in semi-industrial occupations (like the cork-workers in the mountain village of La Garde-Freinet) who were the first to take up arms, and their immediate targets were the local bigwigs – manufacturers, merchants, farmers and the like – who, for their part, armed in support of Napoleon.[22]

In the next revolution, however, and the last in France's nineteenth-century history, the peasants had no role to play at all. The Commune, established in Paris in March 1871, lasted only two months and, though the Parisians won sympathetic support from a number of other towns and cities, half a dozen of which set up short-lived Communes of their own, no serious attempt was made to involve the rural districts until a couple of weeks before Paris fell to the troops of the Federal Government at Versailles (Parisian memories of the peasants' role in June '48 may have had something to do with it). So it was a purely urban affair and, unlike any other revolution in the century, one in which for the first time in history the workers (*prolétaires*) formed a government of their own.

But, more precisely, what sort of government was it? Was it (as Engels defined it in 1891) 'the Dictatorship of the Proletariat';[23] or was it, as Marx called it at the time, 'the political form at last discovered under which to work out the Economic Emancipation of Labour' or (as a variant) 'the harbinger of a new society' – in fact, the 'dicatorship' in embryo

rather than the dictatorship full blown?[24] Whichever formula
we accept (and, for the purposes of this chapter, we are not
obliged to choose one,) there is little doubt that the men and
women who started the revolution by capturing the guns at
Montmartre on 18 March were craftsmen, labourers and their
womenfolk from the parishes close by; and that the Central
Committee of the National Guard, formed some weeks before,
was not far wrong when, two days later, it announced to the
world that 'the proletarians of the Capital [had] taken over the
city'. Moreover, when the Commune was crushed, in late May,
and 36,000 prisoners were taken, of more than 13,000 sentenced
by the military courts to be shot, jailed or transported, the great
majority were craftsmen and labourers; in fact, the wage-
earning element was appreciably greater than it had been
among the prisoners of June 1848. So, in the French vocabulary
of the day (although perhaps not in our own), it is reasonable to
call them '*prolétaires*'. Of the leaders, too, unlike the leaders in
previous revolutions, a large number were workers. Of 81
members of the General Council of the Commune, freely
elected in March (and, therefore as good a yardstick as any), 33
were worker-artisans (mainly of the traditional crafts), 30 were
intellectuals – journalists, doctors, writers, lawyers; 11 were
(white-collar) employees; and, of the rest, 5 were businessmen
and two were professional soldiers.[25] So the social composition,
if not largely proletarian, was overwhelmingly 'popular'.

What do we know of their ideology, of both the leaders and
the followers? The General Council was a mixed bag, drawing
as much on the allegiances of the past as of the present. The most
closely-knit of the larger groups was probably that formed by 34
republican democrats, or neo-Jacobins (Delescluze was the
most 'heroic' example), who looked back to the Committee of
Public Safety of 1793 (Marx had something to say about this,
mostly unflattering). The socialists, or 'socialists', were
therefore, nominally at least, in a majority; but they were split
two ways. There were eleven followers of Blanqui (still in prison
at Versailles), convinced believers in insurrection and
dictatorship, men of action who scorned all compromise and
any idea of planning a new form of society. Twenty-six were
Internationalists, who looked for guidance to the French section
of the Workingmen's International; but these were further
divided between anarchists that followed Proudhon, who had

died a few years before but was still a hero among independent craftsmen and small employers, and Marxist socialists who planned to create a workers' state (but these were in a small minority).[26] Thus composed, it was hardly likely that the Council would take many steps that might lead the Paris workers towards socialism. But, for all its failings and the shortness of its stay in office, the Commune represented a new kind of people's state: it set a maximum on high salaries and wages; it declared a moritorium on evictions; it abolished debts and night working in bakeries; and, above all else, it encouraged popular participation in government, including that of women, to carry out its tasks.

With this, in what sense can one speak of an advance in popular ideology over that of 1830 and 1848? In the sense that many more thousands of workers – and not only the cadres – had been won for socialism (though not always that of the International) and, in spite of the slow growth of factories in Paris, they now saw themselves as *prolétaires*, and no longer as *ouvriers*, let alone as the long forgotten *sans-culottes*. So the capitalist, as the antithesis of the *prolétaire*, was the enemy; but, at a time when large-scale capitalist industry was still in its infancy, particularly in Paris, the 'capitalist' was most often a merchant or a banker and there appeared still to be room for compromise with the 'middling' and professional bourgeoisie. So, to them, the target was not yet the workers' state of the International but it remained the Democratic and Social Republic, which had been so bitterly fought for on the barricades of June and was now, twenty-three years later, under the Commune being realized at last. But, as Marx well understood, the Commune was the 'harbinger of a new society' and not its realization; and, standing between the old and the new with its roots still deeply embedded in the past, we may perhaps describe it as the last of the 'pre-industrial' revolutions rather than as the first of the new.

NOTES

1. L. Chevalier, *La formation de la population parisienne au XIXe siècle*, Paris, 1950; C. H. Pouthas, *La population française pendant la première moitié du XIXe siècle*, Paris, 1956.

2. Edgar Newman, 'The Blouse and the Frock Coat: The Alliance of the Common People of Paris with the Liberal Leadership and the Middle Class during the last Years of the Bourbon Restoration in France', *Journal of Modern History*, xlvi, March 1974, 27.

3. David Pinkney, 'The Crowd in the French Revolution of 1830', *American Hist. Review*, lxx, 1964, 1–17.

4. E. Newman, 'What the Crowd Wanted in the French Revolution of 1830', in *1830 in France*, pp. 17–40.

5. John H. Merriman, 'The Demoiselles of the Ariège, 1829–1831' in *1830 in France*, ed. J. Merriman, New York, 1975, pp. 87–118.

6. For this and much that follows, see Robert Bezucha, *The Lyons Uprising of 1834*, Cambridge, Mass., 1974.

7. *Journal des Débats*, 8 December 1831; cit. Bezucha, p. 48.

8. Bezucha, pp. 148–74, esp. 148, 174.

9. See my *The Crowd in History*, New York, 1964, p. 165.

10. Bernard Moss, 'Parisian Workers and the Origins of Republican Socialism, 1830–33', in Merriman, (ed.), *France in 1830*, pp. 203–17, esp. 211–14.

11. See pp. 29–30, above.

12. *The Recollections of Alexis de Tocqueville*, ed. J. P. Mayer, New York, 1959, pp. 11–12.

13. K. Marx, *Class Struggles in France, 1848–1850*, London, n.d., p. 59; Tocqueville, *Recollections*, pp. 78 ff.

14. *Recollections*, pp. 111–12.

15. Marx, pp. 85–7.

16. *Recollections*, p. 150; Marx, pp. 88–9.

17. Arch. Préf. de Police, Aa429, fo. 441.

18. M. Agulhon, *La République au village (les populations du Var de la Révolution à la Seconde République)*, Paris, 1970, p. 255.

19. Agulhon, *1848 ou l'apprentissage de la République, 1848–1852*, Paris, 1973, p. 108; cit. P. McPhee, 'Popular Culture, Symbolism and Rural Radicalism in Nineteenth-Century France', *Journal of Peasant Studies*, V (2), January 1978, 240.

20. McPhee, p. 239.

21. P. Amann, 'The Changing Outlines of 1848', *American Hist. Review*, lxviii, July 1963, 938–53.

22. *La République au village*, pp. 357–9.

23. F. Engels's Introduction to Marx's *Civil War in France*, German edn., 1891.

24. *Address to the General Council of the International Workingmen's Association on the Civil War in France, 1871*, in *The Paris Commune of 1871. The View from the Left*, ed. E. Schulkind, London, 1972, p. 212.

25. Roger L. Williams, *The French Revolution of 1870–1871*, London, 1969, p. 140.

26. ibid.

Part Four

TRANSITION TO INDUSTRIAL SOCIETY

1

England in the Eighteenth Century

England in the eighteenth century – at least after the turbulent years of Queen Anne – was relatively stable. It would continue to be so until the impact of the French and industrial revolutions began to be felt around the early 1790s. At that point we shall end this chapter and leave the more turbulent years of social history that followed to the next.

Since the Glorious Revolution, which rounded off the struggles between King and Parliament, the country had been ruled by a 'limited' monarchy which became firmly established with the Hanoverian Succession and the muting of the fierce struggles between Whigs and Tories that characterized the reign of Queen Anne. With the limitation of royal authority, sovereignty became divided – at least, so the constitutional lawyers said – between King, Lords and Commons; but, in practice, it was between the Crown and landed aristocracy, which dominated both Houses of Parliament. In fact, society itself was still aristocratic in the sense that the landed interest not only dominated Parliament but also local government, the administration of justice and the patronage of the arts; and it was the aristocracy and gentry, far more than the merchant class or the Hanoverian Court, that imposed its ideology (or its 'hegemony', as Gramsci called it) on all other social groups.

There was, however, an important exception to this general cultural penetration, even among the possessing classes themselves. In the City of London, the merchants and tradesmen had built up over the centuries a bourgeois stronghold of their own; and the present century, in spite of its general freedom from bitter struggles, would witness many a conflict between the City (represented by the plutocratic Court of Aldermen and the more plebeian Court of Common Council) and the King and the majority party in Parliament (by now generally Whig) over trade and economic policy. This conflict over economic interest was reflected in the struggle of political factions; and it was remarkable with what consistency the City –

whether Tory, Whig or 'Radical', as it was in succession – found itself in opposition to the politics of Westminster and St James's between the 1720s and the early 1780s.[1] At that time, as will be seen, the bourgeois interest was represented by the merchant and trading class alone; the manufacturing bourgeoisie was yet to make its appearance as a force to be reckoned with, as we shall see in the following chapter.

At the bottom of the social pyramid, of course, were the labouring or 'popular' classes, few of whom had the vote, but yet, as we shall see, all but the most wretched and abject had, when united, considerable political muscle none the less. In towns and cities they included those whom Daniel Defoe, in a perceptive essay written in 1709, variously defined as the '*working trades*', 'the *poor*' and 'the *miserable*';[2] that is, the small shopkeepers and craftsmen, the unskilled in more or less regular employment, and (in the last group) the 'submerged' class of the chronically poor or sick, the destitute, beggars, vagrants, homeworkers, and many more that Patrick Colqohoun late in the century included among his 'criminal' element. Defoe had added for the countryside 'the *country people*, farmers etc., who fare indifferently'; among these he clearly intended to include the lesser freeholders and yeomanry whereas cottagers and rural labourers belonged among 'the poor'. This would be a fair enough analysis of the poor and labouring population of the early eighteenth century; but, soon after, important social changes came about with the agrarian revolution, which had the effect of eliminating many freeholders and cottagers, of increasing the number of labourers and giving greater substance to many farmers who now ceased to 'fare', so 'indifferently' as before. So, from now on, what remained of the old peasantry began to disappear and the modern-style village – with its tri-part division into squire, farmer and labourer – began to take shape.

For all the relative placidity of the social scene, there was no lack of tension and minor conflict, ranging these dispossessed freeholders, urban craftsmen and wage-earners and small consumers against the possessing classes of merchants, gentry and 'improving' farmers – and occasionally the Government and Parliament itself. For convenience, I will divide this popular protest into four main groups: rural protest; industrial disputes; food (or small consumers') riots; and urban riots of every kind from simple 'tumult' to insurrection. We must look at these in turn and consider the ideology – whether 'inherent' or 'derived' – that infused them.

To begin with rural protest which, as I have suggested, was relatively muted and saw none of the violence that still accompanied old-style peasant rebellion in Eastern Europe, and such as would reappear in France (as we saw in an earlier chapter) once the sixty-year lull was over. In England, too, the rowdy encounters of the century before were a thing of the past. For, to quote E. P. Thompson, 'times and people had changed: the eighteenth century provided *francs-tireurs* of pale-breakers, wood-stealers and poachers, but very rarely any *levée en masse* of the peasantry'.[3] For, in England, the last traces of feudalism in the countryside had been swept away, and capitalist-commercialism had taken its place. Such conflict as there was in the country took place in response to the changes being effected by the agrarian revolution, in the course of which landlords and farmers enclosed fields, built fences, broke up commons and set up turnpikes and toll-gates on the roads; the wealthiest among them set whole parks and forests aside as reserves for game. So the labourers and small tenants responded in kind and pulled down the fences and gates, ploughed up enclosures and invaded the forests for firewood and sport. There were riots against turnpikes in the West Country in 1727, 1735 and 1753 and in the West Riding of Yorkshire the same year; and, in the 1720s, 'King John' and his masked cavaliers ravaged the deer parks at Windsor.[4] Hostility to enclosure was even more sustained: in 1710 in Northampton, in 1758 in Wiltshire and Norwich; but the most rioting occurred after the general Enclosure Act of 1760, which was followed by riots in Northampton and Oxfordshire in 1765, at Boston (Lincs) in 1771, at Worcester in 1772, at Sheffield in 1791 and in the Nottingham district in 1798; there were of course many others not noticed by the press. There was no personal injury done to landlords or farmers and politics played no part in them; the overriding concern was to restore the traditional rights of the village which, the villagers felt, were being sacrificed, with Parliament's support, to the thirst for 'improvement' of landlords and prosperous farmers (whose ideology, quite evidently, was not the same as their own).

Disputes over wages were informed by the same concern for 'justice' and the restoration of a lost right rather than by the ambition to win the wage-earner a larger share of the cake. For, typically, strikes were directed against employers who cut wages to save costs; equally they might arise (as in the extensive riots against the Irish in East London in 1736) in response to the use of cheap labour; or, again, to remove machines that threatened to throw men out of work – of which a comparatively early example was the destruction of Charles Dingley's new mechanical saw-mill in Limehouse in 1768.[5] Such attacks on the employer's property in the course of a dispute were frequent, for at the time it was more usual for strikes to take a violent turn rather than take the form of peaceful marches or petitions. Violence was generally confined to the destruction of the employer's house or machinery; the employer himself was generally left untouched (at the most he might be wheeled off in a barrow or dumped in a pond or ditch, if he ventured to show his face!). 'Scabs' or rival groups of workers were not so lucky, and this was where the bloodshed occurred that marked the London coalheavers' and silk-weavers' strikes of 1768. That year, in fact, was so remarkable for the proliferation of strikes that broke out in the capital, many occurring at about the same time as, and some coinciding with, the height of the political agitation over Wilkes (of which more will be said anon) that one biographer of Wilkes has been prompted to cite them as an early example of 'political' strikes: mistakenly, in my view, as I have attempted to argue elsewhere.[6]

Far more frequent than labour disputes at this time were food riots which, in times of real or anticipated shortage of provisions – particularly of bread – involved all classes of small consumers, wage-earners of course included. Between 1730 and 1795 I have counted 275 food riots out of 375 riots of all kinds reported in the newspapers. Apart from the large numbers of small consumers in any year, it is not surprising that these outbreaks should have been so frequent and to have become more so as the century went on. Bread was the staple diet which, even in normal times, may have accounted for one-third, or even one-half, of the poor man's earnings; bad harvests became more frequent after the 1750s; new methods of distribution were being introduced at about this time, which made it more profitable for the dealers to sell to rich than to poor consumers; and, in addition, there was a long stored-up tradition of popular response to shortage, whether artificial or real, which it only needed a crisis in the food supply – as happened in every decade after the 1740s – to release. According to that tradition, there were a variety of ways in which angry consumers might behave. One was simply to seize the grain without any further ado as it arrived in the market; and there was inevitably a certain amont of uncontrolled looting in all disturbances of the kind. Another was to destroy the grain (presumably as a token form of revenge); and this happened often enough in market riots, particularly in the early decades. A third method was to hold up waggons or convoys, or ships carrying grain to other ports, whether abroad or in parts of the country where grain was in shorter supply. (This appears to have been a more common practice in France, where it was called an '*entrave*', but it was also a frequent occurrence in Cornwall, where the miners marched to the ports to stop the grain; and continued to do so until the 1830s, at least.) The fourth, and most sophisticated form, which required a higher degree of organization to see it through, was the 'setting' or fixing of a 'just price' by the rioters themselves: a form that in France, where it was equally common, was called *la taxation populaire*. This method, while never universal, played an important part in the major late-century riots of 1766, 1795 and 1800–1.[7]

It has been argued that food riots – if they attained a sufficient volume – were often taken over (if not instigated in the first place) by more influential, outside groups and were thus susceptible to the intrusion of political ideas. (We saw an example of this suggestion in a previous chapter when we briefly discussed the French 'flour war' of 1775.) There are cases, of course, where this charge of political collusion appears to have more substance than in others. One such case is that of the grain riots of 1766, which have been studied by a Canadian scholar, Walter Shelton. Dr Shelton has argued that, in these riots the magistrates' sympathy for the rioters and detestation of the dealers helped to prolong the disturbances while a more prompt and determined intervention on their part would have brought them to a speedier conclusion; but he adds that this was by no means typical of the century and that the 'equivocal response of the gentry' betrayed a grievance of their own and was quite peculiar to the occasion.[8] But, basically, the ideology of the food riot was simply the small consumers' concern for the 'just price'; though, as E. P. Thompson has rightly insisted, it was not only the 'justice' of the price that was at issue, but 'justice' in the method of distribution and of operating the market as well; for (to quote him further) popular grievances 'operate within a popular consensus as to what were legitimate practices, and what were illegitimate, in marketing, milling, baking, etc.' This consensus he calls the 'moral economy of the poor'.[9]

Urban riots (particularly those occurring in London) were quite distinctive. For one thing, issues varied widely. They might have to do with food, either taking the form of actual food riots or (as happened in the main year of Wilkite disturbance, 1768) be raised (in the form of slogans, for example) within the context of a wider political movement. Actual food riots were a relatively frequent occurrence in provincial towns, particularly those equipped with an established market: such as Taunton, Aylesbury, Winchester and the like. London was the great exception: it had no food riots at all between 1714 and the mid-1790s. The reason was two-fold: first that London (like Paris) was well provisioned and relatively well policed, the argument being that a riot occurring over bread within easy reach of Whitehall or Westminster would be far more politically dangerous than if it happened elsewhere. The second reason was that London's location (with its protective shield of near-urban Middlesex on its most exposed north-western flank) gave it a degree of immunity from rural 'contamination' that Paris, for example, notoriously lacked. But if London lacked food riots, its role as the centre of government and the hub of the nation's economy made it susceptible to a far wider range of popular disturbance than provincial or market towns. So there were the riots aimed at the Scottish banker, John Law, at the time of the South Sea Bubble (1720); the riots directed at Sir Robert Walpole over Excise in 1733 and over gin in 1736; the commotion over the intention to give easier naturalization to alien Jews in the 1750s; and the riots in support of William Pitt the Elder during the Seven Years War. But these were eclipsed in volume and violence by the enthusiasm aroused by the career of

John Wilkes in the 1760s and seventies, and by the Gordon Riots of 1780, when 'No Popery' crowds held the streets of the capital for a week on end and caused damage to property later assessed for compensation at over £100,000 (a fair sum in those days).[10]

In addition to their variety, London riots naturally tended to be more readily exposed to political influence: this was assured not so much by the proximity of Parliament as by that of the City government, which, as we saw before, played an active role in political affairs. Of the two Courts of City administration, it was the Court of Common Council, the more popular and democratic of the two, that played the leading role in the political education of the 'lower orders' of not only the City itself but, as its political influence extended into a greater metropolis, of large parts of Surrey and Middlesex as well. In the early decades, City politics tended to support Country rather than Court and were therefore Tory rather than Whig; in the 1750s, with the arrival of William Pitt, this switched to a more radical Toryism which, with William Beckford (Pitt's City henchman) and later Wilkes, switched again to a policy critical of both parties and may perhaps be given the label 'radical' as well as any other.[11] And that label, too, may just as reasonably be attached to the activities of the crowds that rallied to 'Wilkes and Liberty' in 1763 and continued to acclaim him and riot in his cause on his return from exile in 1768 and went on doing so until he was finally admitted to Parliament, after his numerous expulsions and disqualifications, in 1774. And even the Gordon Riots, for all the illiberal forms they assumed, were basically cast in a radical mould, drew on a long radical-Protestant tradition and were inspired (if not promoted) by the most radical elements in the city, by men like Frederick Bull, Common Councilman and close friend and ally of Lord George Gordon in the anti-Papist cause.[12]

What, then, was the ideology of the city crowd that distinguished it from that of popular protesters in villages and market towns? Basically, of course, it shared the 'inherent' ideology of crowds elsewhere. It was as much concerned with 'justice' and the rights of the 'freeborn Englishman' as any one else; and the crowds that halloo'ed for Wilkes, as a sign of elementary class hostility to the rich, celebrated their hero's return to Parliament by smashing the windows of lords and

ladies of opulence and fashion on their return from the hustings
at Brentford. This free-and-easy egalitarianism was even more
vividly expressed in the Gordon Riots which, with evident
deliberation, directed their attack against the properties of
prosperous or well-to-do Catholics, while the poor Irish,
though living frequently within easy reach of the rioters, were
left strictly alone. Again, in the Old Bailey *Proceedings* relating to
those brought to trial, we find the case of a man who admitted
that he might have damaged a wealthy Protestant's house, but
(as he told the court): 'Protestant or not, no gentleman need be
possessed of more than £1,000 a year; that is enough for any
gentleman to live upon.'[13]

But, of course, as we have already suggested, the ideology of
the London crowd was something else as well; and the 'derived'
element in city riots is evident for all to see; yet how thoroughly
that element had been absorbed at any particular moment is, of
course, a matter for debate. In the first place, it expressed itself
in slogans, which reflected the political complexion of the City,
or of its 'popular' party, as it changed from one generation to
the next. Examples are the 'High Church and Sacheverell' of the
Tory crowds of 1710; followed by the 'No Excise' of the anti-
Walpole crowd in 1733; 'Wilkes and Liberty', the prevailing
radical slogan of 1763–74; and the 'No Popery' of the Protestant
Association – with strong City support – in June 1780. So while
the slogans and the political complexion they reflected changed
from one major crisis to the next, there was one constant
element: the crowd's mentor was always the City government
(and, most typically, the Court of Common Council), just as in
Paris, before the Revolution, the crowd was most often, when it
came to political issues, given its impetus to act by the
aristocratic Parlement. But how far did the 'instruction' go; how
deeply were the political lessons assimilated by the crowds
which, as fashions changed, rioted for the popular cause of the
day? Or were they simply 'mobs' that responded to the
manipulation of City interests? The question is prompted by
Edward Thompson's charge that I have 'protested too much' in
defending the London or Wilkite crowd against the imputation
of being a mob of hoodlums and 'criminal elements'. He
believes, rather, that the Wilkite crowd, though certainly
sympathetic to Wilkes and not paid to be so, knew that its

violence would not be resisted as it was acting 'under licence' of the City magistrates; and that its volatility became even more evident in the Gordon Riots (following soon after), where its ambivalent behaviour reflected 'a mixture of manipulated mob and revolutionary crowd'. And he concludes that it was 'in fact at a halfway-house in the emergence of popular political consciousness.'[14]

On the whole, I would not quarrel with this conclusion: after all, that 'halfway-house' would still allow for a considerable penetration of political ideas. But it must be added that the outcome of the Gordon Riots proved, to say the least, discouraging for both the crowd and its City mentor. On their own admission, the political back-lash that followed taught the radicals a lesson: as Joseph Brasbridge, a City worthy, put it some time after the excitement was all over: 'From that moment, I shut my ears against the voice of popular clamour';[15] and we know from other evidence that there were many who shared his view. In fact, there was no further question of City or London crowds acting 'under licence' of the Court of Common Council until City radicalism revived, with popular support, in the middle of the Napoleonic Wars.

It remains to consider the common pattern of popular protest at this time – a period, as we have seen, before the industrial revolution had had time to mould the society of England in its image. In the first place, protest was typically marked by direct-action methods and violence to property: strikes developed into riots in which strikers broke machinery, either to save their jobs or to bring their employers to heel through 'collective bargaining by riot';[16] rioters broke into granaries and bakers' shops; and city rioters 'pulled down' their enemy's house or burned him in effigy. But, as we have mentioned before, protest was singularly free from injury to life or limb except in disputes between one group of workers and another; and in other encounters, such blood as was shed was almost always shed by authority: the most notorious example was that of the Gordon Riots as the result of which 285 rioters were shot dead in the streets or died later in hospital and 25 were hanged, while not a single fatality was incurred by the magistrates or troops.

Secondly, in spite of all the destruction of property, great discrimination was shown in selecting targets. In both the

Gordon and Priestley riots (the latter at Birmingham in 1791), rioters picked out the properties to be 'pulled down' with almost uncanny precision (yet none of the 'lists' said to have been carried by leaders have turned up in police or trial records); and, in the first, such non-Catholic houses as were destroyed were either those believed to belong to protectors of Catholics or were the victims of natural forces – as was the case with twenty-five houses in Holborn, adjoining Thomas Langdale's distilleries, which were engulfed by flames, whipped up by a high wind, emanating from the burning liquor stored in their vaults; and many other examples could be cited to support the point.

Thirdly, protest was generally spontaneous, though often, as in food riots, it followed a course dictated by custom. Even in large-scale affrays, like the Wilkite or Gordon Riots, there was the minimum of organization, and disturbance often developed from small beginnings (say, from an angry exchange at a baker's shop or, as in June 1780, from the refusal of a petition by Parliament) into a widespread conflagration and attacks on property. But there were, of course, considerable differences in the degree of spontaneity between urban and rural riots.

Fourthly, leadership: a point that is closely associated with the one before. We might say that, as a general rule, at this time, leadership 'from within' the crowd was still comparatively rare except in short-lived affairs where some persons had a more commanding presence than others or behaved more conspicuously, or were believed to be so, or to do so, by the magistrates or police. But, of course, this depended on the type of disturbance. Turning back to our four categories, the most spontaneous were likely to have been the food riots, where such leaders as later appeared for trial were not so much leaders in any commonly accepted sense of the term as those whose momentary enthusiasm or daring marked them out for arrest by the militia or police. Enclosure riots or attacks on game reserves might be on a small, almost individual, scale; or they might be well organized affairs like the operations carried out in Windsor Park in the 1720s by 'King John' and his fellow-riders. Labour disputes might also take a fairly organized form with elected committees and recognized leaders to conduct operations. This was the case with the hatters, tailors, sailors and silk-weavers, all of whom had committees to run their affairs at the time of the London strikes of 1768. In that year, the silk weavers appear to have been the most highly organized of all: they had collectors to levy dues or to press into membership those who needed coercing; and (most significant of all) two of their committeemen, John Dalline and John Doyle, were arrested and hanged not for taking part in one single event, but for having played a conspicuous role in a series of consecutive affrays. In city riots the case was different again. In the larger affairs there was generally a leader 'from outside' (a Pitt, a Wilkes or a Lord George Gordon), who might be happy enough to be a leader (Wilkes, though he rarely addressed his supporters by word of mouth, was certainly one of these), while others (Gordon is probably an example) had leadership thrust upon them and denied all responsibility for what was done in their name. But there were, in addition to the leaders 'from outside', likely to be short-term leaders or 'mob-captains' from within, or closer to, the crowd, men who enjoyed only a momentary authority and (unlike Doyle and Valline) had no role to play before or after the event. Such men were Matthew Christian, described as 'a gentleman of character and fortune', who was said to have filled the rioters with ale in celebration of Wilkes's election victory in Middlesex in March 1768; and, in the Gordon Riots, a dozen years later, there were men like William Pateman, journeyman wheelwright, and Thomas Taplin, coachmaker, who led bands of rioters or collected money 'for the poor Mob'. From an earlier occasion, mention might also be made of 'Captain Tom the Barber', who, clad 'in a striped Banjan', led anti-Irish rioters in Goodman's Fields in July 1736. (We don't know his proper name, as he preserved his virtual anonymity by evading detection and arrest.)[17]

And, fifth, who were the protesters? In villages, they were smallholders, cottagers, miners and weavers, who are frequently mentioned in food riots as well as in enclosure riots and labour disputes. (Leaders like 'King John', of course – although in no sense from outside, as he participated in the events – was of a higher social status altogether.) In towns, there would be more of a mixture: wage-earners, labourers, servants and apprentices; but also tradesmen, craftsmen and the occasional gentleman (see the case of Matthew Christian). Of course, the composition of the urban crowd varied from one episode to another – as, for example, between the craftsmen and shopkeepers who hallooed for Pitt and the wider spectrum of people of both 'middling' and 'lower sort' – labourers and freeholders as well as craftsmen and shopkeepers – who rioted and huzza-ed for 'Wilkes and Liberty'. But at no point – whether in urban or rural disturbance – may we yet speak of a working class: the industrial revolution was still at too early a stage.

And, finally, to complete the pattern of 'pre-industrial' protest, ideology corresponded broadly to what has been said before: overwhelmingly 'inherent', traditional and apolitical in the case of food riots, strikes and rural protest of every kind; and only touched by the 'derived' ideology of the bourgeoisie – political and forward-looking – in the case of London riots, particularly after the emergence of City radicalism in the mid-fifties. But the forward-looking element was still skin-deep even in such riots, and popular protest, taking the picture as a whole, still looked to the past; or, in E. P. Thompson's phrase, the 'plebeian culture' (admittedly not *exactly* synonymous with my 'ideology') 'is rebellious, but rebellious in defence of custom'.[18]

NOTES

1. L. S. Sutherland, 'The City of London in Eighteenth-Century Politics', in R. Pares and A. J. P. Taylor (eds), *Essays presented to Sir Lewis Namier*, London, 1956, pp. 46–74.

2. Daniel Defoe, *The Review*, 25 June 1709.

3. E. P. Thompson, *Whigs and Hunters: the Origin of the Black Act*, London, 1975, pp. 23–5.

4. ibid., pp. 142–6.

5. See my *Wilkes and Liberty*, Oxford, 1962, pp. 93–4.

6. Raymond Postgate, *That Devil Wilkes*, London, 1956, p. 181; *Wilkes and Liberty*, pp. 103–4.

7. See John Stevenson, 'Food riots, 1792–1818', in J. Stevenson and P. Quinault (eds), *Popular Protest and Public Order*, London, 1974, pp. 33–74; Walter J. Shelton, 'The Role of Local Authorities in the Hunger Riots of 1766', *Albion*, V (1), Spring 1973, 50–66; and Roger Wells, 'The Revolt of the South-West, 1800–1801', *Social History*, no. 6 (October 1977), pp. 713–44.

8. Shelton, loc. cit.

9. E. P. Thompson, 'The Moral Economy of the English Crowd in the Eighteenth Century', *Past and Present*, no. 50, February 1971, pp. 76–136.

10. For further details, see G. Rudé, *The Crowd in History*, New York, 1964, pp. 47–65.

11. See L. S. Sutherland, *The City of London and the Opposition to Government, 1768–1774*, London, 1959, pp.10–11.

12. See my *Paris and London in the Eighteenth Century*, London and New York, 1971, pp. 268–92.

13. ibid., p. 289.

14. E. P. Thompson, *The Making of the English Working Class*, London, 1963, pp. 70–1.

15. Cit. L. S. Sutherland, 'The City of London in Eighteenth-Century Politics', p. 73.

16. E. J. Hobsbawm, 'The Machine Breakers', *Past and Present*, no. 1 (February 1952), pp. 57–70.

17. For the above, see my *Wilkes and Liberty*, p. 44; and *Paris and London . . .*, pp. 79–80, 210. For 'King John' see Thompson, *The Black Act*, pp. 142–6.

18. E. P. Thompson, 'Eighteenth-Century English Society: Class Struggle without Class?', *Social History*, III (2), May 1978, esp. p. 154.

2

Transition to Industrial Society, c. 1800–1850

As was suggested in the last chapter, the transition to industrial society in Britain was ushered in by two events both taking place in the last decades of the eighteenth century: the French and industrial revolutions. The French Revolution, while playing no part at all in the shaping of social change (as it did so dramatically in France), had an important effect on the ideology of popular protest in that it injected it with the twin radical notions of the Rights of Man and the Sovereignty of the People.

But, inevitably, in England it was the industrial revolution that proved to have the greater influence of the two. For not only did it give a new direction to popular protest but it transformed the processes of production and, in so doing, created two new social classes. By the 1820s, factories engaged in the spinning and weaving of cotton – and later in wool and in other branches of manufacture – were displacing the old domestic system, based on the village, and, in the process, were calling into being the two new classes of manufacturing employers, who owned the machines, and of industrial workers who manned them. Thus, through the industrial revolution, society tended to become polarized, as Marx and Engels predicted in the *Manifesto*, between the industrial employing and working classes. But even in England, which became more quickly industrialized than any other country, this process was never completed and left several other classes in being: both a surviving 'challenger' among the former ruling classes and the 'traditional' classes of farmers, shopkeepers and craftsmen that Gramsci wrote of a century later. The surviving 'challenger', the landed class (of which so much was said in our previous chapter), continued to flourish and to play an important, if not still a dominant, role in Parliament and State; but, gradually even its political eminence came to an end and, by the time of the First World War, the Lords had lost their independent status in government and had merged, in all but name (and in the ownership of 'Stately Homes'), with the more powerful bourgeoisie.

However, long before this process of absorption was completed, the manufacturing bourgeoisie, while leaving many of the posts of command to members of the landed class, had become the dominant force in the State. In the period of competitive capitalism, on which our present chapter is focused, the new rulers adopted as their heroes Smith, Malthus and Bentham and, with these as their ideological props, laced with one or other branch of evangelical Christianity, they aimed

(1) to introduce Free Trade and make Britain into the 'workshop of the world' with maximum profits to themselves;

(2) to curb the lingering political domination of aristocracy by parliamentary and local government reform; and

(3) to gain full control of the hiring and firing of labour by keeping workers' 'coalitions' and other impediments to the freedom of trade at bay.

The obstacles standing in the way of realizing these plans were two-fold: first, the landlord class, which clung tenaciously to its corn laws, sinecures and 'rotten' boroughs; but, after 1850, this battle was won and the landlords were becoming the allies, first halfhearted, but later wholehearted, of the bourgeoisie in both economy and government. The second obstacle was more obdurate and could not so easily be appeased; and this chapter – and the next – will be largely concerned with the new central conflict dividing society between employers and workers, a conflict, as we have seen, that played only a secondary role in the century before.

But, before considering how this conflict developed, we must briefly consider the main changes in popular and working-class protest arising from the impact of the 'dual' revolution. First, as we saw, the main protagonists had changed: the typical protesters were no longer the village freeholders, urban craftsmen or small consumers, but now – particularly with the 1830s – the industrial workers, or proletarians, of the new factory towns; nor were the issues propelling them, as so frequently in the past, concerned with the price of bread so much as with the wages in the worker's pocket. Moreover, as industry developed, the *location* of protest moved from South to

North, from village to town, and from old chartered towns to modern industrial cities. The main stages of movement up to the mid-century were roughly as follows:

Stage 1 (early war-years, 1793–1800): marked by 'conspiratorial' Jacobin movements in London, Edinburgh, Manchester (with counter-response from 'Church and King' in Birmingham, Manchester) and by food-rioting in London, south-east England and parts of Wales.

Stage 2 (late war-period, 1811–15): marked by Luddism in the hosiery counties of the Midlands and West Riding of Yorkshire.

Stage 3 (early post-war, 1815–22): marked by general protest in large cities (London, Manchester); centres of declining industry (East Anglia); established ongoing industrial centres (iron districts of South Wales, hosiery counties of Midlands and West Riding); food-rioting in widely scattered market towns (Falmouth, Nottingham, Bolton, Carlisle).

Stage 4 (1829–32): the most tumultuous of all, marked by *a new and decisive shift to the new manufacturing districts* of Midlands, South Wales, North of England and Clydeside; a temporary shift from London to Birmingham and a number of old chartered towns (Nottingham, York, Derby, Bristol); and a final and dramatic upsurge of the rural South (leaving East Anglia and Devon as sole bastions of muted rural protest until agrarian trade unions come along after 1870).

Stage 5 (1830s and 1840s): marked by three main stages of Chartism, spread over mainly industrial Britain and falling into three main geographical divisions: the large and expanding cities (London, Birmingham, Manchester, Glasgow); the new industrial regions of England, Scotland and Wales; and the old dying centres of handloom-weaving and rural industry in the English West Country and the West Riding of Yorkshire. Meanwhile, the more overt agrarian protest has become confined to the 'Celtic fringe' of West Wales and the Scottish Highlands. But, after Chartism, the old centres of handloom weaving and rural industry (having suffered their final defeat) drop out of the picture, and English handloom weavers and Welsh peasant-farmers follow the English peasant-labourers into almost total oblivion; while, on the 'Celtic fringe', only the Scottish Highlands keep up their resistance in the final phase of the Crofters' War.[1]

London in this period is a special case and serves as a reminder that industrialization and urbanization do not necessarily go hand in hand. In the eighteenth century, as we saw, London was the progenitor of popular radicalism and the scene of the most violent and protracted conflicts of the time. But, after the turn of the century, radicalism first moved from the City of London to its periphery, into Westminster and Middlesex, before following industry up to the Midlands and the North. In this period of transition, London only had two brief moments of radical revival, the first over the somewhat 'antiquated' Queen Caroline affair of 1820 (reminiscent of the days of Wilkes),[2] and the second in 1848, when London 'hosted' the People's Charter in its final phase. (There was a further revival of militancy in London in the 1850s and sixties, and again, more vociferously, in the 1880s; but such matters take us beyond the scope of the present chapter.)

With developing industry and commerce, the nature of popular protest also changed and gradually lost the 'pre-industrial' pattern that we described before. The direct-action type of protest began to phase out and gave way (as we shall see) to more organized, and often more *decorous*, forms. First, food riots died out in England after the Napoleonic Wars, after a final fling in East Anglia and a scattering of market towns in 1815–16; after this, they only survived in the 'Celtic fringe', in Cornwall and the Highlands of Scotland. Secondly, machine-breaking virtually ended after industrial Luddism in the Midlands counties between 1811 and 1822 and, in the country, the widespread breaking of threshing machines in 1830–2; and, thirdly, the traditional 'pulling-down' of houses, repeated at Bristol on almost 'No Popery' proportions in 1831, made its final bow on any massive scale in the Pottery towns of Staffordshire in August 1842. Of protest of this type, arson alone survived and remained a feature of agrarian protest until well into the 1860s. (In fact, no fewer than 227 convicted arsonists – among whom, admittedly protesters were almost certainly in a minority – arrived in Western Australia in 1862–6 alone.)[3]

Meanwhile, spontaneity gave way to organization; this was strikingly so with the arrival of the first trade unions recruiting nationally or over a wider field; as with John Dogherty's

National Association for the Protection of the Working Classes, launched in 1830 and claiming 100,000 members in 1831; and, after the short interlude of Owen's strange hybrid, the Grand National Consolidated Trade Union, which fell apart almost as soon as it was started (in 1834), with the highly organized and soundly financed Miners' Association of 1841 and the 'New Model' unions of 1851 on. And with organization came not only the better planning of industrial disputes (making the old type of guerrilla warfare a thing of the past), but also a new type of leader – sometimes a militant like the short-term leaders of the past, and sometimes a 'reformist' who might become later a respectable top-hatted 'gentleman' like the 'New Model' leaders of the 1850s and 1860s. Early examples of the militant type were John Dogherty himself and George Loveless, leader of the Dorchester farm labourers, who was not only transported to Australia as a militant in 1834 but returned one three years later. But all such leaders, whether militant or not, were a product of this period of transition. They were leaders from within the ranks of the workers themselves and no longer either 'from without' or (if 'from within') occasional, anonymous and short-lived like those we discussed in our last chapter, but stable, continuous and openly proclaimed.

Ideology also changed; but, of course, there was no straight line of uninterrupted progress, even among the newly formed industrial working class. The main course of development, however, is clear for all to see, as we saw it before in the case of France: that is, from the beginnings of 'politization' (still largely 'derived') in the 1790s to the period of working-class consciousness beginning in the 1830s (denoting the worker's arrival at the stage of awareness of his place in a class-divided society). We saw in our last chapter the beginnings of a political education among the 'inferior' classes – including shopkeepers of 'the meaner sort', small masters and workers – of urban society. But there was no sign yet of the political education of the workers as a separate social group. This began with the French Revolution though, paradoxically, neither the great *idéologues* of the Revolution nor their greatest spokesman in England, Thomas Paine, had any intention of indoctrinating the workers *as workers*; and we have seen how Paine, when in America, had fallen out with his erstwhile allies among the politically sophisticated craftsmen of Philadelphia because he had shown no inclination to promote their particular interests outside of those of the Patriot body as a whole. So it was in England, where Paine's *Rights of Man*, though widely and enthusiastically read by all the most literate of the industrial workers, had no specific message for the working class. However – and this was the essential novelty as far as the workers were concerned – in England the main promoter of Paine's books and ideas was the London Corresponding Society, formed in 1792 (with 'members unlimited', as E. P. Thompson records), which had the distinction, unique in its day, of being a political society that drew the bulk of its members from among 'mechanics' and working artisans; and it was this body, composed as it was, that directed Paine's teachings on popular sovereignty, human rights and the shortcomings of monarchy and the Established Church above all to the working-class readers of the new industrial towns; and these ideas continued to be read and passed around among weavers, miners and urban craftsmen, openly as long as the law permitted and secretly when the London Corresponding Society and its offshoots in other centres fell victim to Pitt's persecuting war-time measures.

But English Jacobinism, fostered by Paine and the L.C.S., was followed after the wars by a new phase in the English radical reform movement. Cobbett, the one-time scourge of the radical pamphleteers, returned to England from America (bringing Paine's bones with him as a signal mark of repentance), proclaimed himself a radical and gave the old-style Whiggish radicalism a popular face. His great cry was to abolish 'Old Corruption', including rotten boroughs and sinecures; and this was quickly taken up and assimilated by radical artisans, as well as by radicals of other groups, and through them found its way into workers' protest movements, even into such as traditional historians have generally assumed to have confined their activities to purely industrial issues. Luddism is a case in point; and E. P. Thompson is probably the first to have placed Luddism within a wider radical movement for parliamentary reform. And it is from a commentator on Thompson's work that I quote the following passage, evidently Cobbettite in inspiration, taken from an anonymous letter defending the operations of the Nottingham Luddites in 1816:

. . . plunder is not our object, the necessaries of life is what we at present aim for. . . . Perhaps if crowned with success as our services deserve, we may release the kingdoms of our immense load of taxation, an unprecedented National Debt, a corrupt and despotic government, a multiplied train of undeserved sinecures and unmerited pensions. . . .[4]

And more than a dozen years later, during the 'Swing' labourers' movement of 1830, we find John Adams, a radical journeyman shoemaker of Maidstone, leading a 'MOB' of 300 villagers to parley with the Rev. Sir John Filmer of East Sutton Park, opening the discussion by expressing the hope that 'the Gentlemen would go hand in hand with the Labouring Classes to get the expenses of government reduced'; and, the same evening, Mr Gambier, the son of the rector of the neighbouring parish of Langley, was told by Adams and his companions, as an explanation of the labourers' impoverished condition, that 'there were many sinecures'. Others among the labourers' spokesmen had been influenced by Cobbett, too; as, for example, Philip Green, a chimney sweep of Banbury and a one-time sailor, who was described as a great admirer of Cobbett, 'whose productions he is in the habit of quoting in the public houses he frequents'.[5]

But the notion of 'Old Corruption', like its concomitant the 'Norman Yoke', while it did good service to popular radicalism up to early Chartism at least, was essentially backward-looking, looking back to the Good Old Days that Cobbett, with his fear and loathing of the Great Wen, would have dearly wished to spirit back to life. For the first glimmerings of a forward-looking philosophy that was to offer the workers the prospects of a new way of living rather than the restoration of an allegedly better past, we must look to Robert Owen. Owenite socialism, like the 'Utopian' socialism of Cabet and Blanc in France, had plenty of weaknesses; for one thing, it turned its back on political action and pinned its hopes solely on industrial organization and cooperative schemes. But it had virtues that both Painite Jacobinism and Cobbettite radicalism lacked: it invited the workers to come to terms with industrial society and it taught them to believe that it was only through their own efforts that the new cooperative commonwealth would be achieved. These views are echoed in the pamphlet that George Loveless, one-time Owenite and later Chartist, wrote on his return to England from his Australian exile: 'I believe nothing will ever be done to relieve the distress of the working classes unless they take it into their own hands; with these views I left England, and with these views I am returned.'[6]

There was still a long way to go before arriving at working-class consciousness, which could not long survive without a place being found for both political and industrial action. Chartism, though it was full of contradictions, blending new and old forms and ideas (as we shall see), was an essential step in this process. For the first time, the workers themselves (and not only small cadres of craftsmen and tradesmen as in 1792) took the initiative in launching a nationwide movement to establish a new type of Parliament to be elected by workers and to be composed of the workers' own representatives. This in itself would have been novel enough, but Chartism aspired to far more than that: it aimed through the vote to protect the workers' communities from disruption by capitalist 'improvers' and to win for them all those solid social benefits that one of its leaders, the Rev. J. R. Stephens, lumped together under the title of a 'knife-and-fork' question. It was only through such a merger of economic and political action that the English workers, like the French, could hope to attain an awareness of being a class; but only provided the Chartist campaign for the Charter was accompanied by parallel action in the workshops and mines. Here, as we know, Chartism proved a dismal failure and went down to defeat (though not on this score alone). Yet Chartism's failure was by no means complete; for the great battles fought out in the North in the summer of 1842 – particularly in Lancashire's industrial towns – battles with employers, army and 'new' police – proved to be of immense value in forging the working-class movement of the future.

Somewhat on the fringe of Chartism, John Foster, a young scholar, has recently argued,[7] a body of industrial workers, located in one single Lancashire town, went forward to attain that working-class consciousness for which all previous workers' movements and radical indoctrination were a form of preparation. But working-class consciousness, John Foster argues, could not be simply based on the advent of a new ideology – socialism, for example – but on (what Chartism generally failed to achieve) a mixture of radical ideas and militant working-class action in the factory or shop. For the appearance of this phenomenon he looks at three English industrial towns of the 1830s and forties, all three having much in common: Oldham, a Lancashire cotton town; South Shields, a ship-building centre in Durham; and Northampton, centre of the Midlands boot and shoe trade. But, of the three, Oldham alone comes up to the mark whereas both Northampton and South Shields are described (in the style of Georg Lukács) as remaining 'falsely conscious'. And why this separation between the sheep and goats? Because, as Foster shows, the workers of Oldham had, from the early 1830s on, developed a long and continuous record of combining militancy in the factory or on the shop floor with political militancy in promoting, through such political means as were available to them, radical candidates to represent them in local government and Parliament; whereas in South Shields and Northampton the workers limited their militancy to industrial action and tough talk at the employers, while neglecting to take care of the political side; that is, they suffered from the 'economism' that Lenin so sadly deplored in *What is to be Done?*

But, Foster continues, the conditions governing Oldham's class consciousness changed before 1848; and from now on Oldham, too, like South Shields and Northampton, lapsed into 'false' consciousness. We shall say more about this phenomenon and the reasons that brought it about in the following chapter.[8]

As Foster's example of Oldham further shows, the road to a profound change in working-class ideology was a steep and thorny one and Lenin's famous law of the 'uneven development of capitalism' could as aptly be applied to the evolution of working-class consciousness in nineteenth-century Britain. All through this period, when profound changes were taking place – say, from the early 1820s – some groups of workers and some parts of England forged ahead and others lagged behind; and often the old and new were found uneasily balanced within the same political movement; none of which, of course, is particularly surprising if we consider the survival of those older 'traditional' classes of which we spoke before. Chartism is a good example of such a movement and presents an excellent case-study for the uneven process of transition to an industrial society. This is personified in the Chartist leadership, among whom there was all the difference in the world between Jacobins like Julian Harney and radical Tories like Feargus O'Connor who looked to the past, and champions of trade unionism like Peter McDouall or new-style socialists like Ernest Jones, who corresponded with Marx. These contrasts are equally reflected in the activities in which Chartism engaged, varying from one region to the next. On the one hand, there were the Chartist petitions, borrowed from a radical past but looking forward to the future; the National Charter Association, the forerunner of a 'labour' party; and the workers' organized industrial movement in the Manchester district; and, on the other, there was the Land Plan through which O'Connor, for whom industrialism and urban growth were anathemas, aimed to solve society's ills by putting back on the land those whom capitalism had made redundant; and there were also the machine-breaking activities of the 'Plug-Plot' rioters who ran berserk in the Staffordshire pottery towns.

If industrial protest thus mingled the old with the new, rural protest remained far more resistant to change. Throughout the period, old-style forms, infused with an old-style ideology, continued – like the East Anglian rural riots over wages, machines and the price of bread in 1816; the machine-breaking activities of the 'Swing' riots in the southern counties in 1830; and the strange millenarial episode of the Kentish labourers who fought to the death in defence of their self-styled Messiah, the spurious Sir William Courtenay, in 1838. The movement of the Dorset labourers – the 'men of Tolpuddle' – who set up a branch of Owen's Grand National union in 1834, was something quite different; for this was the offspring of Owenite agitation emanating from Birmingham and was, therefore, properly speaking, not a genuine labourers' movement at all. These movements (apart from the last) were informed by an 'inherent' or traditional ideology as well: the rioters of 1816 were wholly concerned with a 'just price' and a 'just wage'. The 'Swing' rioters of 1830 burned barns and broke machines to restore the 'just wage' that labour-saving farmers and landlords, through the use of machines, were threatening to undermine further than they had done already by misuse of the Poor Law; and they appealed to traditional authority, to the magistrates, and even to the King or to God himself, to restore the lost rights of which they believed they had been robbed. In September 1831, a machine-breaker arrested at Dilham, in Norfolk, told the court that sentenced him to two years in prison, in terms reminiscent of the Puritan Revolution, that 'in destroying machinery, I am doing God a service' (and there were magistrates who said the same in other words).[9] Again, in the Potteries riots of 1842, a man seen putting a piano on the fire, in the course of a disturbance at Longton, near Stoke-on-Trent, told an onlooker that 'the Lord was at his side, and the flames would not hurt him'.[10] In the village, in fact, the real change did not come until the 1860s.

On the 'Celtic fringe' it might take even longer. Food riots lingered on in Cornwall until the 1830s, at least; and they continued in the Highlands until the great 'famine' of 1847. Turnpike riots which, in England, barely outlasted the Napoleonic Wars, survived in North and West Wales into the 1840s. For two years between 1839 and 1842, Rebecca and her 'Daughters', with blackened faces and heavy skirts, rode down turnpikes and tollgates along the country roads of Carmarthen, Pembroke and Glamorgan.[11] In the Highlands, the crofters, with memories still fresh of the Clearances of more than half-a-century before, kept up the struggle against landlords, factors, magistrates, police and 'alien' ministers of the Church by direct-action means (though with a minimum of violence) until the 1880s: in Inverness-shire, in particular, where there were over 200 commitments for riot and assaults on the police between 1885 and 1888; that is, even after the last great episode in the Crofters' War, the so-called 'Battle of the Braes', was fought out on the island of Skye in 1882.[12]

NOTES

1. For a fuller presentation of this changing geographical pattern of protest, see my *Protest and Punishment*, Oxford, 1978, pp. 31–8.
2. For 'The Queen Caroline Affair', see J. Stevenson, in John Stevenson (ed.), *London in the Age of Reform*, Oxford, 1977, pp. 117–48.
3. Rudé, *Protest and Punishment*, p. 230.
4. 'The Secretary of the Black Committee of the Independent Luddites of Nottinghamshire Division' to R. Newcombe and Son, 11 November 1816,

P.R.O., H.O. 42/155; cited by F. K. Donnelly, 'Ideology and early English Working-class History: Edward Thompson and his Critics', *Social History*, no. 2, May 1976, p. 226. But, of course, from the style, this is more likely to be the work of an educated sympathizer holding Cobbettite radical views than that of a Luddite workingman. But, whether 'genuine' or not, it appears to be a piece of 'derived' middle-class radical ideology, typical of pre-industrial, pre-proletarian, popular radicalism.

5. Hobsbawm and Rudé, *Captain Swing*, pp. 102–3, 143.

6. G. Loveless, *The Victims of Whiggery*, London, 1837.

7. J. Foster, *Class Struggle and the Industrial Revolution. Early Industrial Capitalism in Three English Towns*, London, 1974.

8. But it must be said that Foster, while basing his argument on the Lukácsian model, does not give the same finality to the state of 'false consciousness' as his mentor appears to do. In Lukács, there is in practice little hope for salvation for those who fail to make the grade once the opportunity is offered. But, in Foster, 'false' and 'true' consciousness, like other conditions of man, develop – and decline – historically; that is, both depend on the circumstances prevailing rather than on the absolute or merely partial conversion to right-minded ideas. Therefore, 'false' consciousness has, by human endeavour under the right circumstances, the possibility of being converted (or re-converted) into 'true' or 'class' consciousness (Foster, *Class Struggle*, esp. pp. 4–6).

9. *East Anglian*, 25 October 1831.

10. *Annual Register*, vol. 84 (1842), p. 134.

11. David Williams, *The Rebecca Riots; A Study in Agrarian Discontent*, Cardiff, 1953.

12. 'Return of Offences committed in Crofting Parishes in the Highlands and Islands of *Scotland*, arising out of Disputes in regard to the Right to Land, or the Rent of Land, during and since 1874', PP 1888, lxxxii, 2–9. See also Eric Richards, 'Patterns of Highland Discontent 1790–1860', in J. Stevenson and R. Quinault (eds), *Popular Protest and Public Order*, London, 1974.

3

Postscript: Industrial Britain

In previous chapters we have written of popular ideology in terms of development from a lower to a higher stage of consciousness; so that in each chapter we have seen the common people – the workers or peasants – enriching their ideology through indoctrination, experience or struggle. In this, our last, chapter the presentation has to be a different one; for we shall be concerned with failure rather than success and consider why the workers' movement in England, after the end of Chartism, went through a long period of lull (what Engels called its 'forty-years' winter sleep') followed by a brief revival in the 1880s before continuing along a zigzag path of victory and defeat. This roughly has been the pattern of the past hundred years.

First, we must consider the mid-century defeat. How was it possible for the high hopes raised by Chartism and the class consciousness of the Oldham workers (as described by Foster) in the 1830s and 1840s to collapse so utterly by the 1850s? The most common, and the basic, explanation has been that British capitalism, from being in a state of continuous crisis and disruption in the 'hungry forties' and the years preceding, began to become stabilized and that Britain, after the Repeal of the Corn Laws, through Free Trade and commercial supremacy became, as is known, the 'Workshop of the World'. So it was able to deliver the goods, not only by distributing greater wealth among the possessing classes but among wider sections of the people as a whole. This, in itself, it has been argued, played an important part in defusing popular militancy; and Marx, as he watched foreign investments pouring into Britain in the 1850s, described the process aptly as 'the rock on which the Counter-Revolution built its church'.[1] Engels had certainly failed to anticipate the situation when he wrote his *Condition of the Working Class*; but he acknowledged in a later Introduction (in 1892) that prosperity had rubbed off on the factory workers, in particular, thus averting the revolution he had foreseen over a generation earlier.[2] And Emile Halévy, the great exponent of the theory of religion as a stabilizing factor in Britain's early nineteenth century, agreed that, on this occasion, it was prosperity rather than religion that played the larger part: writing of England in 1852, he observed that 'we have no longer any need to seek, as we sought in our first volume [concerned with England in 1815] outside the economic sphere the explanation of the stability and balance of such a society'.[3]

But such natural factors as sudden economic prosperity could only hope to give the process of 'de-fusing' a good start: another economic crisis (which no one could be sure of averting) might incite the workers to further acts of militancy; and this, as we have suggested, was rarely the case over the next thirty to forty years. Something more positive had to be devised by the capitalists and the Government that shared in their spoils in order to ensure that the submissive mood of the workers should not be a purely transitory phenomenon. Emigration to Canada and Australia seemed a possible solution and had the advantage of according with the still popular Malthusian principles; though it is doubtful if the attempt thereby to ship militants abroad had, in fact, the desired result. (*Punch*, with its cartoon of a poverty-stricken Chartist worker being lured to emigrate, apparently believed it should.) Another means was the orchestration of propaganda to teach men – socialist men, in particular – the error of their ways; and the late 1840s saw the emergence of a crop of class 'mutualists' and propagandists for social peace. The Christian Socialists – F. D. Maurice, Charles Kingsley and Thomas Hughes – played their part by preaching cooperation through Christian fraternity; and even the one-time firebrand, Thomas Carlyle, wrote his *Latter-Day Pamphlets* appealing to employers to give their workers 'fair play' so that they might win their cooperation in return.[4]

Also growing out of this situation – whether by chance or by design – is what has been called the 'aristocracy of labour'. Though differing in their explanations of its origins, historians have agreed that the 'aristocracy' was a privileged upper crust of industrial workers whose effect, or purpose, was to disarm the workers ideologically and thus help the employers to maintain stability and social peace. They were distinguished in some cases by their higher wages, easily awarded in a period of steeply rising profits, and, in all cases, by their policies – if leaders or other opinion-formers – of class cooperation whether through the ballot or in the workship. Some historians (including Hobsbawm and Foster) have seen them as an emanation of the 1840s and 1850s, while others have followed Lenin more closely by linking them rather with the Imperialism that followed a generation later.[5] If one is to accept the former rather than the latter view (and for the purposes of this chapter the difference is of no great importance), it would seem that none had a greater claim to the title (though in this case we are applying it to a group of leaders rather than to the workers they helped to shape) than the famous 'Junta' of Allan, Applegarth, Odger and a handful of others who, over a period of years, dominated the affairs of the New Model trade unions of the 1850s and sixties. Apart from their positive achievements and innovations (which were of some importance to the general history of trade unionism), the Webbs describe how 'they accepted, with perfect good faith, the economic Individualism of their middle-class opponents, and claimed only that freedom to combine which the more enlightened members of that class were willing to concede to them'.[6] And Robert Applegarth, summoned to appear before the Royal Commission on Trade Unions in 1867, outlined the conditions governing admission to his union (the Amalgamated Society of Carpenters and Joiners) as follows:

> He must be in good health, have worked five years in the trade, be a good workman, of steady habits, of good moral character, and not more than 45 years of age.[7]

While he does not deny the importance of a growing national prosperity as a major means of de-fusing working-class militancy, John Foster insists that most of the other means involved in the process were quite deliberately devised by the capitalist class (either severally or collectively) in order to restabilize both society and industry. He calls this process one of 'liberalization', and he describes how it began to be operated in Oldham some time in the 1840s. It took various forms: the introduction of wages differentials to divide the workers; the deliberate isolation of the workers at large from their hitherto respected vanguard by making half-concessions; the adoption by bourgeois politicians of the ten-hour day in order to make the inevitable compromise more acceptable; and the 'adoption' of the workers' militant policies by Tories and Cobbettites in order to water them down; as at Oldham in 1852, when they issued a joint manifesto offering their support for a 10-hour day and opposition to the poor law, coupled with a declaration of the need to 'preserve a just balance between capital and labour, and especially to protect the labouring classes against the cruel machinations of a false political economy'.[8]

Yet more was needed to give this employer-worker partnership greater durability: to disrupt the old divisive tendencies towards a working-class consciousness and implant in its place what Trygve Tholfsen calls 'a cohesive culture – a highly knit structure of values: institutions, roles and rituals'; and he describes how it became largely possible over a period of twenty years to replace 'a culture pervaded by social tension' by one of 'shared values, internalized and institutionalized'. He goes on to describe its main ingredients as

(a) the ethic of individual improvement and advancement through hard work, labour discipline and thrift – with joint participation of workers and employers expressing 'shared goals';
(b) the 'moral elevation' of the working classes as a continuous objective; and
(c) the cultivation of personal virtues and personal salvation, including total abstinence.

The means whereby such ideas were fostered and given circulation were varied enough: workingmen's clubs, newspapers, Sunday Schools, Mechanics' Institutes, Mutual Improvement Societies, Reading Rooms, Libraries, Savings Banks, churches and chapels were all assigned to play a role. Ideas of this kind spread with great speed. Tholfsen cites a number of examples, including that of a workingmen's club at Newcastle which, in 1865, stated among its objectives 'the social intercourse, mutual help, mental and moral improvement, rational recreation and amusement of its members'.[10] Yet, he argues, the surrender to a capitalist ideology was not so complete as it might seem. For one thing, there was no slavish adoption by the workers of all aspects of middle-class values such as those promoted by *laissez-faire* propaganda along the lines of Samuel Smiles; and he quotes the *Beehive* newspaper in 1860 as accompanying its exhortation to seek 'emancipation of the working men through 'self-improvement' with a blistering exposure of the evils of competition. Moreover, the germs of the workers' surrender to middle-class values were already in being and were being preached by the Radicals themselves in the course of the Chartist movement. He cites, in particular, the example of an Owenite branch in Huddersfield in 1844, which advertised 'classes for mutual improvement . . . to develop each other's moral, social and sympathetic feelings'; and a Chartist circular of 1841, which ran as follows:

> And though we admit that *class legislation* has inflicted upon us ills innumerable, and blighted the intellect and broken the hearts of whole generations of sons of toil, we cannot shut our eyes to the truth THAT NO STATE OF FREEDOM CAN IMPROVE THE MAN WHO IS THE SLAVE OF HIS OWN VICES.[11]

So there were elements, during the previous period of working-class militancy, in the Chartist schools and the like, which, by placing self-improvement and personal salvation high on their order of priorities, prepared the way for the later surrender to a bourgeois hegemonic culture and made it all the easier and less painful for the workers to swallow. Nor should it be supposed that concern for 'improvement' need, in the long run, be such a grave disadvantage to the future of the workers' movement. For such qualities accorded well with a concern for careful organization and the husbanding of resources, qualities that had been conspicuously lacking in such ephemeral enterprises as the Owenite National Consolidated Trade Union of twenty years before. The New Model leaders taught different lessons, and for all their respectability and imitation of middle-class manners and values, they made a positive contribution for the future by building solid national organizations for the craftsmen and miners, at least, and left a useful heritage for their successors to put to good effect. This period of high respectability, it should also be remembered, saw the creation of the London Trades Council and the Trades Union Congress; and in 1872 Joseph Arch launched the first great national organization of farm workers; and he, too, like the Allans and Applegarths of the generation before, remained all his life a staunch upholder of 'self-help and liberty', 'order and progress'.[12]

It might, in fact, be argued that the propagation of middle-class values after the mid-1840s, though it served to arrest the growth of working-class consciousness in the industrial districts, did not prove an unmitigated evil. Moreover, the Victorian 'cultural stability' that they helped to create was in its turn undermined by the succession of crises in both agriculture and industry that followed the first great challenge to Britain's industrial and commercial supremacy from Germany and the United States in the mid-1870s to the late 1880s. The crises led to massive unemployment and to deep dissatisfaction, leading in turn to the first serious attempt to organize the unskilled workers (gasworkers and dockers)[13] and the first serious penetration of the trade unions by Marxist-socialist ideas. It was at this time (in the early 1890s) that William Morris, a member of the recently-founded Socialist Society, said that the real business of a socialist party was to foster and extend a real socialist consciousness among working men, 'so that they may at last . . . understand themselves to be face to face with a false society, themselves the only possible elements of true society'.[14] And when, on May Day 1890, the British trade unions, sweeping aside the objections of the diehards of 'old' unionism, joined the first International May Day celebrations, held in London in support of the 8-hour day, Engels wrote of it as an event of capital importance, for (he wrote) 'on 4 May 1890, the *English proletariat*, newly wakened from its forty-years' winter sleep, *again entered the movement of its class*. . . . The grandchildren of the old Chartists are entering the line of battle.'[15]

But the hopes this roused among socialists were short-lived. The crisis that brought in 'new' unionism, the revival of socialism and the agitation for an eight-hour day also saw the rise of the new Imperialism or Scramble for Empire in which Britain joined alongside its German, French, Russian (and later American) rivals. And Imperialism – as Cecil Rhodes and Joseph Chamberlain had hoped – gave many British workers the same sense of security and superiority over their fellow-workers overseas as the knowledge that Britain was commercially superior to the rest of the world had done at the time of the Great Exhibition of two generations before. Of course, the realization that the fruits of Empire were unevenly distributed between the classes broke through in times of economic crisis – as in 1911–14, 1920–2 and 1926; but, in spite of the promise of 1890, the continuing absence of socialist 'theory' within the labour movement (as Engels had noted) severely limited class perception; and when, at the time of the Persian oil crisis of 1950, Ernest Bevin, Labour's Foreign Secretary, boasted that it was Empire that assured the British workers of a privileged economic position, there were few to dispute the claim.

Though the Empire has continued to disintegrate, it has taken time for century-old convictions to become dispelled. But although the curse of colonialism and the memories of by-gone glories continue to haunt a solid core of diehards in the movement, it would be wrong to claim (as might be claimed by upholders of the notion of a Wall of Babylon dividing the 'falsely' from the 'truly' conscious) that all is therefore lost. For the workers have long memories of both victories and defeats, and there are limits to the ability of even the most alluring of alien propaganda to alter deeply-felt beliefs and attitudes; and there is a great deal of truth in Richard Hoggart's conclusion to the picture he paints of the effects on the working-class of Leeds of the 'candy-floss' press and other insidious onslaughts of the consumer society of the 1950s: 'The working classes have a strong natural ability to survive change *by adapting or assimilating what they want in the new and ignoring* the rest.'[16]

This is reassuring as far as it goes; but the discerning reader may note that it is another of those 'inherent' attitudes which have, in themselves, proved insufficient to win decisive battles. For this, as we have seen, the ideology of the common people – whether composed of peasants, workers or *menu peuple* – has had to be reinforced by an injection of 'derived' ideas, or of those generalized ideas based on the memory of past struggles to which Marx and Engels, writing on separate occasions, quite simply gave the name of 'theory'.

NOTES

1. Cit. R. B. Smith, in *Labour History*, Canberra, November 1971, p. 82.
2. F. Engels, *The Condition of the English Working Class in 1844*, Introduction to 1st Eng. edition, London, 1892.
3. E. Halévy, *A History of the English People*, IV, 337; cit. Trygve R. Tholfsen, 'The Intellectual Origins of Mid-Victorian Stability', *Polit. Sci. Quart.*, LXXXVI (March 1971), 58 (n. 2).
4. R. B. Smith, loc. cit.
5. H. F. Moorhouse, 'The Marxist Theory of the Labour Aristocracy', *Social History*, II (January 1978), 61–82.
6. S. and B. Webb, *The History of Trade Unionism*, London, 1896, p. 221.
7. First Report, Royal Commission on Trade Unions, PP 1867, XLV (8), 12–13; cit. L. Evans and P. Pledger (eds), *Contemporary Sources and Opinions in Modern British History*, 2 vols, Melbourne, 1967, II, 40–2.
8. Foster, *Class Struggle . . .* , pp. 203 ff.
9. Tholfsen, p. 61.
10. ibid., pp. 63–4.
11. ibid., p. 68.
12. J. P. D. Dunbabin, *Rural Discontent in Nineteenth-Century Britain*, London, 1974, p. 262.
13. For the significance of the Dock Strike of 1889 in bringing discipline, organization and purpose to London's 'casual poor' after the wild orgy of the riots of 1886, see Gareth Stedman Jones, *Outcast London*, Oxford, 1971, pp. 315–21.
14. Cit. A. L. Morton (ed.), *Political Writings of William Morris*, pp. 232–3.
15. F. Engels, in the Vienna *Arbeiterzeitung*, 13 May 1890; cit. in K. Marx and F. Engels, *Selected Correspondence 1846–1895*, D. Torr (ed.), London, 1934, p. 469.
16. R. Hoggart, *The Uses of Literacy*, London, 1957, p. 52 (my italics).

Bibliography

Titles are distributed according to the Part in which they are cited most frequently or (if not actually cited) to which they are considered most relevant.

Part One   Ideology and Class Consciousness

Althusser, L., *Lenin and Philosophy and Other Essays*, London, 1971.

Althusser, L., *Politics and History*, London, 1972.

Anderson, Perry, *Considerations on Western Marxism*, London, 1973.

Colletti, L., *From Rousseau to Lenin*, London, 1972.

Geertz, C., 'Ideology as a Cultural System', in *Ideology and Discontent*, ed. D. E. Apter, New York, 1967.

Hill, C., 'The Norman Yoke', in *Democracy and the Labour Movement*, ed. J. Saville, London, 1954.

Hobsbawm, E. J., *Primitive Rebels*, Manchester, 1959.

Lenin, V. I., *What is to be Done?*, London, 1927.

Lewis, O., 'The Culture of Poverty', *Scientific American*, CCXI (1966), 19–25.

Lichtheim, G., *The Concept of Ideology and other Essays*, New York, 1967.

Lukács, G., *History and Class Consciousness*, London, 1971.

Mannheim, K., *Ideology and Utopia*, London, 1936.

Marx, K., *A Contribution to the Critique of Political Economy*, Moscow, 1951.

Marx, K. and Engels, F., *The German Ideology*, London, 1974.

Marx, K. and Engels, F., *The Holy Family, or Critique of Critical Criticism*, Moscow, 1975.

Marx, K. and Engels, F., *The Manifesto of the Communist Party* (various editions).

Marx-Engels Selected Correspondence, 1846–1895, ed. D. Torr, London, 1934.

Mornet, D., *Les origines intellectuelles de la Révolution française*, Paris, 1933.

On Ideology, Working Papers in Cultural Studies 10, University of Birmingham, 1977.

Plamenatz, J., *Ideology*, London 1970.

Political Writings of William Morris, ed. A. L. Morton, London, 1973.

Raab, F., *The English Face of Machiavelli*, London, 1964.

Rogers, P. G., *Battle in Bossenden Wood*, London, 1961.

Sanderson, M., 'Literacy and Social Mobility in the Industrial Revolution in England', *Past and Present*, no. 56, August 1972, pp. 75–104.

Selections from the Prison Notebooks of Antonio Gramsci, ed. Q. Hoare and G. Nowell Smith, London, 1971.

Stone, L., 'Literacy and Education in England, 1640–1900', *Past and Present*, no. 42, February 1969, pp. 69–139.

Thompson, E. P., 'Eighteenth-Century English Society: Class Struggle without Class?', *Social History*, III (2), May 1978, 137–65.

Thompson, E. P., 'The Moral Economy of the English Crowd of the Eighteenth Century', *Past and Present*, no. 50, May 1971, pp. 76–136.

Weber, Max, *The Protestant Ethic and the Spirit of Capitalism*, London, 1930.

Part Two   Peasants

Bak, J. (ed.), *The German Peasant War of 1525*: Special Issue of *Journal of Peasant Studies*, iii (1), October 1975.

Blum, J., *The End of the Old Order in Rural Europe*, Princeton, 1978.

Cambridge Medieval History, vol. VII.

Cohn, Henry, 'The Peasants of Swabia, 1525', *Journal of Peasant Studies*, iii (1), October 1975, 10–28.

Cumberland, C., *Mexico: The Struggle for Modernity*, New York, 1968.

Engels, F., *The Peasant War in Germany*, London, 1967.

Foster, R. and Greene, J. P. (eds), *Pre-Conditions of Revolution in Early Modern Europe*, Baltimore, 1970.

Herbert, S., *The Fall of Feudalism in France*, New York, 1969 (reprint).

Hilton, R. H., 'Peasants, Peasant Society, Peasant Movements and Feudalism in Medieval Europe', in Henry A. Landsberger (ed.), *Rural Protest*, pp. 67–94 (below).

Hobsbawm, E. J., 'Peasant Movements in Colombia', *International Journal of Economic and Social History*, no. 8 (1976), pp. 166–86.

Huizer, G., and Stavenhagen, K., 'Peasant Movements and Land Reform in Latin America', in Landsberger (ed.), *Rural Protest*, pp. 378–409.

Journal of Peasant Studies (JPS), vol. 1–3 (1973–6): various short items on Brazil, Colombia, Ecuador, Bolivia, Mexico, Peru, etc., under rubric 'Peasants Speak'.

Joutard, Philippe, 'La Cévenne camisarde', *Histoire* (Paris), no. 1, May 1978, pp. 54–63.

Labrousse, C.-E., Introduction to *La Crise de l'économie française à la fin de l'Ancien Régime et au début de la Révolution*, Paris, 1944.

Landsberger, B. and H., 'The English Peasant Revolt of 1381', in H. Landsberger (ed.), *Rural Protest* (below), pp. 95–141.

Landsberger, Henry A. (ed.), *Rural Protest: Peasant Movements and Social Change*, London, 1974.

Lefebvre, G., *Etudes sur la Révolution française*, Paris, 1954.

Lewin, Linda, 'The Oligarchical Limitations of Social Banditry in Brazil', *Past and Present*, no. 82, February 1979, pp. 116–46.

Link, E. M., *The Emancipation of the Austrian Peasant 1740–1798*, London, 1949.

Longworth, P., 'The Pugachev Revolt. The last Great Cossack Uprising', in H. Landsberger (ed.), *Rural Protest*, pp. 194–258.

Moore, Barrington, *Social Origins of Dictatorship and Democracy*, Boston, 1966.

Mousnier, R., *Peasant Uprisings in Seventeenth-Century France, Russia and China*, London, 1971.

Nicolas, J., 'Sur les émotions populaires au XVIIIe siècle: le cas de la Savoie', *Annales historique de la Révolution française*, no. 214, 1973, pp. 593–607; no. 215, 1974, pp. 111–53.

Petit-Dutaillis, C., *Les soulèvements des travailleurs d'Angleterre en 1381*, Paris, 1895.

Porchnev, B., *Les soulèvements populaires en France au XVIIe siècle*, Paris, 1972.

Portal, R., *L'Oural au XVIIIe siècle*, Paris, 1950.

Raeff, M., 'Pougachev's Rebellion', in Foster and Greene, *Pre-conditions* (above).

Rudé, G., *The Crowd in History*, New York, 1964.

Salmon, J. N. M., 'Venal Office and Popular Sedition in Seventeenth-Century France', *Past and Present*, no. 37, 1967, pp. 21–43.

Shanin, T. (ed.), *Peasants and Peasant Societies*, Penguin, 1971.

Tannenbaum, F., *The Mexican Agrarian Revolution*, New York, 1928.

Trevelyan, G. M., *England in the Age of Wycliffe*, London, 1899.

Wangermann, E., *From Joseph II to the Jacobin Trials*, Oxford, 1959.

Wolf, E., *Peasants*, New York, 1966.

Wolf, E., *Peasant Wars of the Twentieth Century*, New York, 1969.

Womack, J., *Zapata and the Mexican Revolution*, London, 1968.

Part Three   Revolutions

Agulhon, M., *1848 ou l'apprentissage de la République, 1848–1852*, Paris, 1973.

Agulhon, M., *La République au village*, Paris, 1970.

Amann, P., 'The Changing Outlines of 1848', *American Historical Review*, LXVIII (July 1963), 938–53.

Baylin, B., *The Ideological Origins of the American Revolution*, Harvard, 1967.

Bezucha, R., *The Lyons Uprising of 1834*, Camb. Mass., 1974.

Chevalier, L., *La formation de la population parisienne au XIXe siècle*, Paris, 1950.

Cobban, A., *The Social Interpretation of the French Revolution*, London, 1964.

Countryman, E., '"Out of the Bounds of the Law". Northern Land Rioters in the Eighteenth Century', in A. Young (ed.), *The American Revolution* (below).

Ernst, J., '"Ideology" and an Economic Interpretation of the Revolution', in A. Young (ed.), *The American Revolution* (below).

Faure, E., *La disgrâce de Turgot*, Paris, 1961.

Foner, E., 'Tom Paine's Republic: Radical Ideology and Social Change', in A. Young (ed.), *The American Revolution* (below).

Garden, M., *Lyon et les lyonnais au XVIIIe siècle*, Paris, 1970.

Gauthier, F., *La voie paysanne dans la Révolution française; l'exemple de la Picardie*, Paris, 1977.

Hill, C. (ed.), *Winstanley, The Law of Freedom and other Essays*, London, 1973.

Hill, C., *The World Turned Upside Down*, London/New York, 1972.

Hoerder, D., 'Boston Leaders and Boston Crowds, 1765–1776', in A. Young (ed.), *The American Revolution* (below).

Jaurès, J., *Histoire socialiste de la Révolution française*, A. Soboul (ed.). 7 vols, Paris, 1968–73.

Lefebvre, G., *The Coming of the French Revolution*, Princeton, 1947.

Lemisch, J., 'Jack Tar in the Street. Merchant Seamen in the Politics of Revolutionary America', *William and Mary Quarterly*, 25 (1968), 371–407.

Macpherson, C. B., *The Political Theory of Possessive Individualism*. Oxford, 1962.

Maier, P., *From Resistance to Revolution*. New York, 1972.

Mandrou, R., *De la culture populaire aux 17e et 18e siècles*. Paris, 1964.

Manning, B., *The English People and the English Revolution*. Penguin, 1978.

Marx, K., *The Civil War in France*, London, 1933.

Marx, K., *Class Struggles in France, 1848–50*, London, n.d.

Mathiez, A., *Le Club des Cordeliers pendant la crise de Varennes et le massacre du Champ de Mars*, Paris, 1910.

Mathiez, A., *Les grandes journées de la Constituante*, Paris, 1913.

Merriman, J. (ed.), *1830 in France*, New York, 1975.

Moss, B., 'Parisian Workers and the Origins of Republican Socialism, 1830–33', in Merriman (above).

Nash, G., 'Social Change and the Growth of Pre-revolutionary Urban Radicalism', in A. Young (ed.), *The American Revolution* (below).

Newman, E., 'The Blouse and the Frockcoat', *Journal of Modern History*, xlvi (March 1974), 27 ff.

Pinkney, D., 'The Crowd in the French Revolution of 1830', *American History Review*, lxx (1964), 1–17.

Pouthas, C. H., *La population française pendant la première moitié du XIXe siècle*, Paris, 1956.

Recollections of Aléxis de Tocqueville, ed. J. P. Mayer, New York, 1959.

Robbins, C., *The Eighteenth-Century Commonwealthman*, Cambridge, Mass., 1959.

Rouff, M., 'Une grève de gagne-deniers en 1786 à Paris', *Revue Historique*, clxv (1910), 332–46.

Rudé, G., *The Crowd in the French Revolution*, Oxford, 1959.

Rudé, G., 'Revolution and Popular Ideology', in M. Allain and G. R. Conrad (eds), *France and North America: The Revolutionary Experience*, Lafayette (Louisiana), 1974.

Schulkind, E. (ed.), *The Paris Commune of 1871. The View from the Left*, London, 1972.

Soboul, A., *The Parisian Sans-Culottes and the French Revolution 1793–4*, Oxford, 1964.

Thönnesson, K. D., *La défaite des sans-culottes*, Oslo, 1959.

Vovelle, M., 'Le tournant des mentalités en France 1750–1789; la sensibilité pré-révolutionnaire', *Social History*, May 1977, pp. 605–29.

Williams, R., *The French Revolution of 1870–1871*, London, 1969.

Young, Alfred (ed.), *The American Revolution. Explorations in the History of American Radicalism*, DeKalb, 1976.

Young, Arthur, *Travels in France during the Years 1787–1788–1789*. J. Kaplow (ed.), New York, 1969.

Part Four Transition to Industrial Society

Donnelly, F. K., 'Ideology and Early Working-Class History: Edward Thompson and his Critics', *Social History*, no. 2, May 1976.

Dunbabin, J. P. D., *Rural Discontent in Nineteenth-Century Britain*. London, 1974.

Engels, F., *The Condition of the English Working Class in 1844*, London, 1892.

Foster, J., *Class Struggle and the Industrial Revolution*. London, 1974.

Hobsbawm, E. J., *Labouring Men*, London, 1969.

Hobsbawm, E. J., 'The Machine-Breakers', *Past and Present*, no. 1, February 1952, pp. 57–70.

Hobsbawm, E. J. and Rudé, G., *Captain Swing*, London, 1969.

Hoggart, R., *The Uses of Literacy*, London, 1957.

Loveless, G., *The Victims of Whiggery*, London, 1837.

McBriar, A. M., *Fabian Socialism and English Politics 1884–1918*, Cambridge, 1962.

Moorhouse, H. F., 'The Marxist Theory of the Labour Aristocracy', *Social History*, II (January 1978), 61–82.

Postgate, R., *That Devil Wilkes*, London, 1956.

Rudé, G., *Paris and London in the Eighteenth Century*, London/New York, 1971.

Rudé, G., *Protest and Punishment*, Oxford, 1978.

Rudé, G., *Wilkes and Liberty*, Oxford, 1962.

Shelton, W., 'The Role of the Local Authorities in the Hunger Riots of 1766', *Albion*, v (1), Spring 1973, pp. 50–66.

Stedman Jones, G., *Outcast London*, Oxford, 1971.

Stevenson, J., 'Food Riots of 1792–1818', in J. Stevenson and P. Quinault (eds), *Popular Protest and Public Order*, London, 1974, pp. 33–74.

Stevenson, J. (ed.), *London in the Age of Reform*, London, 1977.

Sutherland, L. S., 'The City of London in Eighteenth-Century Politics', in R. Pares and A. J. P. Taylor (eds), *Essays presented to Sir Lewis Namier*, London, 1956, pp. 49–74.

Sutherland, L. S., *The City of London and the Opposition to Government 1768–1774*, London, 1959.

Tholfsen, T. R., 'The Intellectual Origins of Mid-Victorian Stability', *Political Sciences Quarterly*, LXXXVI (March 1971), 57–91.

Thompson, E. P., *Whigs and Hunters: the Origins of the Black Act*, London, 1975.

Thompson, E. P., *The Making of the English Working Class*, London, 1962.

Thompson, E. P., 'The Moral Economy of the English Crowd in the Eighteenth Century', *Past and Present*, no. 50, February 1971, pp. 76–136.

Webb, S. and B., *The History of Trade Unionism*, London, 1896.

Wells, R., 'The Revolt of the South-West, 1800–1801', *Social History*, no. 6, October 1977, pp. 713–44.

Williams, D., *The Rebecca Riots: A Study in Agrarian Discontent*, Cardiff, 1953.

Williams, R., *Culture and Society 1780–1950*, London, 1958.

Index